THIRD EDITION

RESUMES FOR

BUSINESS MANAGEMENT CAREERS

The Editors of McGraw-Hill

New York   Chicago   San Francisco   Lisbon   London   Madrid   Mexico City
Milan   New Delhi   San Juan   Seoul   Singapore   Sydney   Toronto

Library of Congress Cataloging-in-Publication Data

Resumes for business management careers / the editors of McGraw-Hill.—3rd ed.
p.   cm.
ISBN 0-07-146780-7 (alk. paper)
1. Resumes (Employment)   2. Cover letters.   3. Executives—United States.   I. McGraw-Hill Companies.

HF5383.V46   2006
650.14'2—dc22   2006043810

1 2 3 4 5 6 7 8 9 10 11 12 13 14 15 QPD/QPD   0 9 8 7 6

ISBN-13: 978-0-07-146780-3
ISBN-10:   0-07-146780-7

McGraw-Hill books are available at special quantity discounts to use as premiums and sales promotions, or for use in corporate training programs. For more information, please write to the Director of Special Sales, Professional Publishing, McGraw-Hill, Two Penn Plaza, New York, NY 10121-2298. Or contact your local bookstore.

Contents

Introduction

Your resume is your first impression on a prospective employer. Though you may be articulate, intelligent, and charming in person, a poor resume can prevent you from having the opportunity to demonstrate your interpersonal skills because it can prevent you from being called for an interview. While few people are hired solely on the basis of their resume, a well-written, well-organized resume can go a long way toward helping you land an interview. Your resume's main purpose is to get you that interview. The rest is up to you and the employer. If you both feel that you are right for the job and the job is right for you, chances are you will be hired.

A resume must catch the reader's attention yet still be easy to read and to the point. Resume styles have changed over the years. Today, brief and focused resumes are preferred. Employers no longer have the patience, or the time, to review several pages of solid type. A resume should be only one page long, if possible. Time is a precious commodity in today's business world, and the resume that is concise and straightforward will usually be the one that gets noticed.

Don't assume, however, that because you are writing a brief resume you can take less care in preparing it. A successful resume takes time and thought, and if you are willing to make the effort, the rewards are well worth it. Think of your resume as a sales tool. You want to sell yourself to a prospective employer. This book is designed to help you prepare a resume that will further your career by helping you to land that next job, or first job, or to return to the workforce after years of absence. So, read on. Make the effort and reap the rewards that a strong resume can bring to your career. Let's get to it!

The Elements of an Effective Resume

An effective resume is composed of information that employers are most interested in knowing about a prospective job applicant. This information is conveyed by a few essential elements. The following is a list of elements that are found in most resumes—some essential, some optional. Later in this chapter, we will further examine the role of each of these elements in the makeup of your resume.

- Heading

- Objective and/or Keyword Section

- Work Experience

- Education

- Honors

- Activities

- Certificates and Licenses

- Publications

- Professional Memberships

- Special Skills

- Personal Information

- References

The first step in preparing your resume is to gather information about yourself and your past accomplishments. Later you will refine this information, rewrite it using effective language, and organize it into an attractive layout. But first, let's take a look at each of these important elements individually so you can judge their appropriateness for your resume.

Heading

Although the heading may seem to be the simplest section of your resume, be careful not to take it lightly. It is the first section your prospective employer will see, and it contains the information she or he will need to contact you. At the very least, the heading must contain your name, your home address, and, of course, a phone number where you can be reached easily.

In today's high-tech world, many of us have multiple ways that we can be contacted. You may list your e-mail address if you are reasonably sure the employer makes use of this form of communication. Keep in mind, however, that others may have access to your e-mail messages if you send them from an account provided by your current company. If this is a concern, do not list your work e-mail address on your resume. If you are able to take calls at your current place of business, you should include your work number, because most employers will attempt to contact you during typical business hours.

If you have voice mail or a reliable answering machine at home or at work, list its number in the heading and make sure your greeting is professional and clear. Always include at least one phone number in your heading, even if it is a temporary number, where a prospective employer can leave a message.

You might have a dozen different ways to be contacted, but you do not need to list all of them. Confine your numbers or addresses to those that are the easiest for the prospective employer to use and the simplest for you to retrieve.

Objective

When seeking a specific career path, it is important to list a job or career objective on your resume. This statement helps employers know the direction you see yourself taking, so they can determine whether your goals are in line with those of their organization and the position available. Normally, an objective is one to two sentences long. Its contents will vary depending on your career field, goals, and personality. The objective can be specific or general, but it should always be to the point. See the sample resumes in this book for examples.

If you are planning to use this resume online, or you suspect your potential employer is likely to scan your resume, you will want to include a "keyword" in the objective. This allows a prospective employer, searching hundreds of resumes for a specific skill or position objective, to locate the keyword and find your resume. In essence, a keyword is what's "hot" in your particular field at a given time. It's a buzzword, a shorthand way of getting a particular message across at a glance. For example, if you are a lawyer, your objective might state your desire to work in the area of corporate litigation. In this case, someone searching for the keyword "corporate litigation" will pull up your resume and know that you want to plan, research, and present cases at trial on behalf of the corporation. If your objective states that you "desire a challenging position in systems design," the keyword is "systems design," an industry-specific shorthand way of saying that you want to be involved in assessing the need for, acquiring, and implementing high-technology systems. These are keywords and every industry has them, so it's becoming more and more important to include a few in your resume. (You may need to conduct additional research to make sure you know what keywords are most likely to be used in your desired industry, profession, or situation.)

There are many resume and job-search sites online. Like most things in the online world, they vary a great deal in quality. Use your discretion. If you plan to apply for jobs online or advertise your availability this way, you will want to design a scannable resume. This type of resume uses a format that can be easily scanned into a computer and added to a database. Scanning allows a prospective employer to use keywords to quickly review each applicant's experience and skills, and (in the event that there are many candidates for the job) to keep your resume for future reference.

Many people find that it is worthwhile to create two or more versions of their basic resume. You may want an intricately designed resume on high-quality paper to mail or hand out *and* a resume that is designed to be scanned into a computer and saved on a database or an online job site. You can even create a resume in ASCII text to e-mail to prospective employers. For further information, you may wish to refer to the *Guide to Internet Job Searching*, by Frances Roehm and Margaret Dikel, updated and published every other year by McGraw-Hill. This excellent book contains helpful and detailed information about formatting a resume for Internet use. To get you started, in Chapter 3 we have included a list of things to keep in mind when creating electronic resumes.

Although it is usually a good idea to include an objective, in some cases this element is not necessary. The goal of the objective statement is to provide the employer with an idea of where you see yourself going in the field. However, if you are uncertain of the exact nature of the job you seek, including an objective that is too specific could result in your not being considered for a host of perfectly acceptable positions. If you decide not to use an objective heading in your resume, you should definitely incorporate the information that would be conveyed in the objective into your cover letter.

Work Experience

Work experience is arguably the most important element of them all. Unless you are a recent graduate or former homemaker with little or no relevant work experience, your current and former positions will provide the central focus of the resume. You will want this section to be as complete and carefully constructed as possible. By thoroughly examining your work experience, you can get to the heart of your accomplishments and present them in a way that demonstrates and highlights your qualifications.

If you are just entering the workforce, your resume will probably focus on your education, but you should also include information on your work or volunteer experiences. Although you will have less information about work experience than a person who has held multiple positions or is advanced in his or her career, the amount of information is not what is most important in this section. How the information is presented and what it says about you as a worker and a person are what really count.

As you create this section of your resume, remember the need for accuracy. Include all the necessary information about each of your jobs, including your job title, dates of employment, name of your employer, city, state, responsibilities, special projects you handled, and accomplishments. Be sure to list only accomplishments for which you were directly responsible. And don't be alarmed if you haven't participated in or worked on special projects, because this section may not be relevant to certain jobs.

The most common way to list your work experience is in *reverse chronological order*. In other words, start with your most recent job and work your way backward. This way, your prospective employer sees your current (and often most important) position before considering your past employment. Your most recent position, if it's the most important in terms of responsibilities and relevance to the job for which you are applying, should also be the one that includes the most information as compared to your previous positions.

Even if the work itself seems unrelated to your proposed career path, you should list any job or experience that will help sell your talents. If you were promoted or given greater responsibilities or commendations, be sure to mention the fact.

The following worksheet is provided to help you organize your experiences in the working world. It will also serve as an excellent resource to refer to when updating your resume in the future.

WORK EXPERIENCE

Job One:

Job Title _____

Dates _____

Employer _____

City, State _____

Major Duties _____

_____

_____

_____

_____

_____

_____

_____

Special Projects _____

_____

_____

_____

Accomplishments _____

_____

_____

_____

_____

_____

Job Two:

Job Title _____

Dates _____

Employer _____

City, State _____

Major Duties _____

_____

_____

_____

_____

_____

_____

_____

Special Projects _____

_____

_____

_____

Accomplishments _____

_____

_____

_____

_____

_____

_____

_____

Job Three:

Job Title _____

Dates _____

Employer _____

City, State _____

Major Duties _____

_____

_____

_____

_____

_____

_____

Special Projects _____

_____

_____

_____

Accomplishments _____

_____

_____

_____

_____

_____

_____

_____

Job Four:

Job Title _____

Dates _____

Employer _____

City, State _____

Major Duties _____

_____

_____

_____

_____

_____

_____

Special Projects _____

_____

_____

_____

Accomplishments _____

_____

_____

_____

_____

_____

_____

Activities

Perhaps you have been active in different organizations or clubs; often an employer will look at such involvement as evidence of initiative, dedication, and good social skills. Examples of your ability to take a leading role in a group should be included on a resume, if you can provide them. The activities section of your resume should present neighborhood and community activities, volunteer positions, and so forth. In general, you may want to avoid listing any organization whose name indicates the race, creed, sex, age, marital status, sexual orientation, or nation of origin of its members because this could expose you to discrimination. Use the following worksheet to list the specifics of your activities.

ACTIVITIES

Organization/Activity _____

Accomplishments _____

_____

_____

Organization/Activity _____

Accomplishments _____

_____

_____

Organization/Activity _____

Accomplishments _____

_____

_____

As your work experience grows through the years, your school activities and honors will carry less weight and be emphasized less in your resume. Eventually, you will probably list only your degree and any major honors received. As time goes by, your job performance and the experience you've gained become the most important elements in your resume, which should change to reflect this.

Certificates and Licenses

If your chosen career path requires specialized training, you may already have certificates or licenses. You should list these if the job you are seeking requires them and you, of course, have acquired them. If you have applied for a license but have not yet received it, use the phrase "application pending."

License requirements vary by state. If you have moved or are planning to relocate to another state, check with that state's board or licensing agency for all licensing requirements.

Always make sure that all of the information you list is completely accurate. Locate copies of your certificates and licenses, and check the exact date and name of the accrediting agency. Use the following worksheet to organize the necessary information.

CERTIFICATES AND LICENSES

Name of License _____

Licensing Agency _____

Date Issued _____

Name of License _____

Licensing Agency _____

Date Issued _____

Name of License _____

Licensing Agency _____

Date Issued _____

Publications

Some professions strongly encourage or even require that you publish. If you have written, coauthored, or edited any books, articles, professional papers, or works of a similar nature that pertain to your field, you will definitely want to include this element. Remember to list the date of publication and the publisher's name, and specify whether you were the sole author or a coauthor. Book, magazine, or journal titles are generally italicized, while the titles of articles within a larger publication appear in quotes. (Check with your reference librarian for more about the appropriate way to present this information.) For scientific or research papers, you will need to give the date, place, and audience to whom the paper was presented.

Use the following worksheet to help you gather the necessary information about your publications.

PUBLICATIONS

Title and Type (Note, Article, etc.) _____

Title of Publication (Journal, Book, etc.) _____

Publisher _____

Date Published _____

Title and Type (Note, Article, etc.) _____

Title of Publication (Journal, Book, etc.) _____

Publisher _____

Date Published _____

Title and Type (Note, Article, etc.) _____

Title of Publication (Journal, Book, etc.) _____

Publisher _____

Date Published _____

Professional Memberships

Another potential element in your resume is a section listing professional memberships. Use this section to describe your involvement in professional associations, unions, and similar organizations. It is to your advantage to list any professional memberships that pertain to the job you are seeking. Many employers see your membership as representative of your desire to stay up-to-date and connected in your field. Include the dates of your involvement and whether you took part in any special activities or held any offices within the organization. Use the following worksheet to organize your information.

PROFESSIONAL MEMBERSHIPS

Name of Organization _____

Office(s) Held_____

Activities _____

Dates _____

Name of Organization _____

Office(s) Held_____

Activities _____

Dates _____

Name of Organization _____

Office(s) Held_____

Activities _____

Dates _____

Name of Organization _____

Office(s) Held_____

Activities _____

Dates _____

Special Skills

The special skills section of your resume is the place to mention any special abilities you have that relate to the job you are seeking. You can use this element to present certain talents or experiences that are not necessarily a part of your education or work experience. Common examples include fluency in a foreign language, extensive travel abroad, or knowledge of a particular computer application. "Special skills" can encompass a wide range of talents, and this section can be used creatively. However, for each skill you list, you should be able to describe how it would be a direct asset in the type of work you're seeking because employers may ask just that in an interview. If you can't think of a way to do this, it may be extraneous information.

Personal Information

Some people include personal information on their resumes. This is generally not recommended, but you might wish to include it if you think that something in your personal life, such as a hobby or talent, has some bearing on the position you are seeking. This type of information is often referred to at the beginning of an interview, when it may be used as an icebreaker. Of course, personal information regarding your age, marital status, race, religion, or sexual orientation should never appear on your resume as personal information. It should be given only in the context of memberships and activities, and only when doing so would not expose you to discrimination.

References

References are not usually given on the resume itself, but a prospective employer needs to know that you have references who may be contacted if necessary. All you need to include is a single sentence at the end of the resume: "References are available upon request," or even simply, "References available." Have a reference list ready—your interviewer may ask to see it! Contact each person on the list ahead of time to see whether it is all right for you to use him or her as a reference. This way, the person has a chance to think about what to say *before* the call occurs. This helps ensure that you will obtain the best reference possible.

Writing Your Resume

Now that you have gathered the information for each section of your resume, it's time to write it out in a way that will get the attention of the reviewer—hopefully, your future employer! The language you use in your resume will affect its success, so you must be careful and conscientious. Translate the facts you have gathered into the active, precise language of resume writing. You will be aiming for a resume that keeps the reader's interest and highlights your accomplishments in a concise and effective way.

Resume writing is unlike any other form of writing. Although your seventh-grade composition teacher would not approve, the rules of punctuation and sentence building are often completely ignored. Instead, you should try for a functional, direct writing style that focuses on the use of verbs and other words that imply action on your part. Writing with action words and strong verbs characterizes you to potential employers as an energetic, active person, someone who completes tasks and achieves results from his or her work. Resumes that do not make use of action words can sound passive and stale. These resumes are not effective and do not get the attention of any employer, no matter how qualified the applicant. Choose words that display your strengths and demonstrate your initiative. The following list of commonly used verbs will help you create a strong resume:

administered	assembled
advised	assumed responsibility
analyzed	billed
arranged	built

carried out	inspected
channeled	interviewed
collected	introduced
communicated	invented
compiled	maintained
completed	managed
conducted	met with
contacted	motivated
contracted	negotiated
coordinated	operated
counseled	orchestrated
created	ordered
cut	organized
designed	oversaw
determined	performed
developed	planned
directed	prepared
dispatched	presented
distributed	produced
documented	programmed
edited	published
established	purchased
expanded	recommended
functioned as	recorded
gathered	reduced
handled	referred
hired	represented
implemented	researched
improved	reviewed

saved	supervised
screened	taught
served as	tested
served on	trained
sold	typed
suggested	wrote

Let's look at two examples that differ only in their writing style. The first resume section is ineffective because it does not use action words to accent the applicant's work experiences.

WORK EXPERIENCE
Regional Sales Manager

Manager of sales representatives from seven states. Manager of twelve food chain accounts in the East. In charge of the sales force's planned selling toward specific goals. Supervisor and trainer of new sales representatives. Consulting for customers in the areas of inventory management and quality control.

Special Projects: Coordinator and sponsor of annual Food Industry Seminar.

Accomplishments: Monthly regional volume went up 25 percent during my tenure while, at the same time, a proper sales/cost ratio was maintained. Customer-company relations were improved.

In the following paragraph, we have rewritten the same section using action words. Notice how the tone has changed. It now sounds stronger and more active. This person accomplished goals and really *did* things.

WORK EXPERIENCE
Regional Sales Manager

Managed sales representatives from seven states. Oversaw twelve food chain accounts in the eastern United States. Directed the sales force in planned selling toward specific goals. Supervised and trained new sales representatives. Counseled customers in the areas of inventory management and quality control. Coordinated and sponsored the annual Food Industry Seminar. Increased monthly regional volume by 25 percent and helped to improve customer-company relations during my tenure.

One helpful way to construct the work experience section is to make use of your actual job descriptions—the written duties and expectations your employers have for a person in your current or former position. Job descriptions are rarely written in proper resume language, so you will have to rework them, but they do include much of the information necessary to create this section of your resume. If you have access to job descriptions for your former positions, you can use the details to construct an action-oriented paragraph. Often, your human resources department can provide a job description for your current position.

The following is an example of a typical human resources job description, followed by a rewritten version of the same description employing action words and specific details about the job. Again, pay attention to the style of writing instead of the content, as the details of your own experience will be unique.

WORK EXPERIENCE
Public Administrator I

Responsibilities: Coordinate and direct public services to meet the needs of the nation, state, or community. Analyze problems; work with special committees and public agencies; recommend solutions to governing bodies.

Aptitudes and Skills: Ability to relate to and communicate with people; solve complex problems through analysis; plan, organize, and implement policies and programs. Knowledge of political systems, financial management, personnel administration, program evaluation, and organizational theory.

WORK EXPERIENCE
Public Administrator I

Wrote pamphlets and conducted discussion groups to inform citizens of legislative processes and consumer issues. Organized and supervised 25 interviewers. Trained interviewers in effective communication skills.

After you have written out your resume, you are ready to begin the next important step: assembly and layout.

Chapter 3

Assembly and Layout

A t this point, you've gathered all the necessary information for your resume and rewritten it in language that will impress your potential employers. Your next step is to assemble the sections in a logical order and lay them out on the page neatly and attractively to achieve the desired effect: getting the interview.

Assembly

The order of the elements in a resume makes a difference in its overall effect. Clearly, you would not want to bury your name and address somewhere in the middle of the resume. Nor would you want to lead with a less important section, such as special skills. Put the elements in an order that stresses your most important accomplishments and the things that will be most appealing to your potential employer. For example, if you are new to the workforce, you will want the reviewer to read about your education and life skills before any part-time jobs you may have held for short durations. On the other hand, if you have been gainfully employed for several years and currently hold an important position in your company, you should list your work accomplishments ahead of your educational information, which has become less pertinent with time.

Certain things should always be included in your resume, but others are optional. The following list shows you which are which. You might want to use it as a checklist to be certain that you have included all of the necessary information.

Essential	Optional
Name	Cellular Phone Number
Address	Pager Number
Phone Number	E-Mail Address or Website Address
Work Experience	Voice Mail Number
Education	Job Objective
References Phrase	Honors
	Special Skills
	Publications
	Professional Memberships
	Activities
	Certificates and Licenses
	Personal Information
	Graphics
	Photograph

Your choice of optional sections depends on your own background and employment needs. Always use information that will put you in a favorable light—unless it's absolutely essential, avoid anything that will prompt the interviewer to ask questions about your weaknesses or something else that could be unflattering. Make sure your information is accurate and truthful. If your honors are impressive, include them in the resume. If your activities in school demonstrate talents that are necessary for the job you are seeking, allow space for a section on activities. If you are applying for a position that requires ornamental illustration, you may want to include border illustrations or graphics that demonstrate your talents in this area. If you are answering an advertisement for a job that requires certain physical traits, a photo of yourself might be appropriate. A person applying for a job as a computer programmer would *not* include a photo as part of his or her resume. Each resume is unique, just as each person is unique.

Types of Resumes

So far we have focused on the most common type of resume—the *reverse chronological* resume—in which your most recent job is listed first. This is the type of resume usually preferred by those who have to read a large number of resumes, and it is by far the most popular and widely circulated. However, this style of presentation may not be the most effective way to highlight *your* skills and accomplishments.

For example, if you are reentering the workforce after many years or are trying to change career fields, the *functional* resume may work best. This type of resume puts the focus on your achievements instead of the sequence of your work history. In the functional resume, your experience is presented through your general accomplishments and the skills you have developed in your working life.

A functional resume is assembled from the same information you gathered in Chapter 1. The main difference lies in how you organize the information. Essentially, the work experience section is divided in two, with your job duties and accomplishments constituting one section and your employers' names, cities, and states; your positions; and the dates employed making up the other. Place the first section near the top of your resume, just below your job objective (if used), and call it *Accomplishments* or *Achievements*. The second section, containing the bare essentials of your work history, should come after the accomplishments section and can be called *Employment History*, since it is a chronological overview of your former jobs.

The other sections of your resume remain the same. The work experience section is the only one affected in the functional format. By placing the section that focuses on your achievements at the beginning, you draw attention to these achievements. This puts less emphasis on where you worked and when, and more on what you did and what you are capable of doing.

If you are changing careers, the emphasis on skills and achievements is important. The identities of previous employers (who aren't part of your new career field) need to be downplayed. A functional resume can help accomplish this task. If you are reentering the workforce after a long absence, a functional resume is the obvious choice. And if you lack full-time work experience, you will need to draw attention away from this fact and put the focus on your skills and abilities. You may need to highlight your volunteer activities and part-time work. Education may also play a more important role in your resume.

The type of resume that is right for you will depend on your personal circumstances. It may be helpful to create both types and then compare them. Which one presents you in the best light? Examples of both types of resumes are included in this book. Use the sample resumes in Chapter 5 to help you decide on the content, presentation, and look of your own resume.

Resume or Curriculum Vitae?

A curriculum vitae (CV) is a longer, more detailed synopsis of your professional history, which generally runs three or more pages in length. It includes a summary of your educational and academic background as well as teaching and research experience, publications, presentations, awards, honors, affiliations, and other details. Because the purpose of the CV is different from that of the resume, many of the rules we've discussed thus far involving style and length do not apply.

A curriculum vitae is used primarily for admissions applications to graduate or professional schools, independent consulting in a variety of settings, proposals for fellowships or grants, or applications for positions in academia. As with a resume, you may need different versions of a CV for different types of positions. You should only send a CV when one is specifically requested by an employer or institution.

Like a resume, your CV should include your name, contact information, education, skills, and experience. In addition to the basics, a CV includes research and teaching experience, publications, grants and fellowships, professional associations and licenses, awards, and other information relevant to the position for which you are applying. You can follow the advice presented thus far to gather and organize your personal information.

Special Tips for Electronic Resumes

Because there are many details to consider in writing a resume that will be posted or transmitted on the Internet, or one that will be scanned into a computer when it is received, we suggest that you refer to the *Guide to Internet Job Searching*, by Frances Roehm and Margaret Dikel, as previously mentioned. However, here are some brief, general guidelines to follow if you expect your resume to be scanned into a computer.

- Use standard fonts in which none of the letters touch.

- Keep in mind that underlining, italics, and fancy scripts may not scan well.

- Use boldface and capitalization to set off elements. Again, make sure letters don't touch. Leave at least a quarter inch between lines of type.

- Keep information and elements at the left margin. Centering, columns, and even indenting may change when the resume is optically scanned.

- Do not use any lines, boxes, or graphics.

- Place the most important information at the top of the first page. If you use two pages, put "Page 1 of 2" at the bottom of the first page and put your name and "Page 2 of 2" at the top of the second page.

- List each telephone number on its own line in the header.

- Use multiple keywords or synonyms for what you do to make sure your qualifications will be picked up if a prospective employer is searching for them. Use nouns that are keywords for your profession.

- Be descriptive in your titles. For example, don't just use "assistant"; use "legal office assistant."

- Make sure the contrast between print and paper is good. Use a high-quality laser printer and white or very light colored 8½-by-11-inch paper.

- Mail a high-quality laser print or an excellent copy. Do not fold or use staples, as this might interfere with scanning. You may, however, use paper clips.

In addition to creating a resume that works well for scanning, you may want to have a resume that can be e-mailed to reviewers. Because you may not know what word processing application the recipient uses, the best format to use is ASCII text. (ASCII stands for "American Standard Code for Information Interchange.") It allows people with very different software platforms to exchange and understand information. (E-mail operates on this principle.) ASCII is a simple, text-only language, which means you can include only simple text. There can be no use of boldface, italics, or even paragraph indentations.

To create an ASCII resume, just use your normal word processing program; when finished, save it as a "text only" document. You will find this option under the "save" or "save as" command. Here is a list of things to *avoid* when crafting your electronic resume:

- Tabs. Use your space bar. Tabs will not work.

- Any special characters, such as mathematical symbols.

- Word wrap. Use hard returns (the return key) to make line breaks.

- Centering or other formatting. Align everything at the left margin.

- Bold or italic fonts. Everything will be converted to plain text when you save the file as a "text only" document.

Check carefully for any mistakes before you save the document as a text file. Spellcheck and proofread it several times; then ask someone with a keen eye to go over it again for you. Remember: the key is to keep it simple. Any attempt to make this resume pretty or decorative may result in a resume that is confusing and hard to read. After you have saved the document, you can cut and paste it into an e-mail or onto a website.

Layout for a Paper Resume

A great deal of care—and much more formatting—is necessary to achieve an attractive layout for your paper resume. There is no single appropriate layout that applies to every resume, but there are a few basic rules to follow in putting your resume on paper:

- Leave a comfortable margin on the sides, top, and bottom of the page (usually one to one and a half inches).

- Use appropriate spacing between the sections (two to three line spaces are usually adequate).

- Be consistent in the *type* of headings you use for different sections of your resume. For example, if you capitalize the heading EMPLOYMENT HISTORY, don't use initial capitals and underlining for a section of equal importance, such as Education.

- Do not use more than one font in your resume. Stay consistent by choosing a font that is fairly standard and easy to read, and don't change it for different sections. Beware of the tendency to try to make your resume original by choosing fancy type styles; your resume may end up looking unprofessional instead of creative. Unless you are in a very creative and artistic field, you should almost always stick with tried-and-true type styles like Times New Roman and Palatino, which are often used in business writing. In the area of resume styles, conservative is usually the best way to go.

CHRONOLOGICAL RESUME

LUIS CASTILLO
8155 N. Knox
Billings, MT 59101
(708) 555-3168
luiscastillo@xxx.com

WORK EXPERIENCE:
Gateway, Inc., Billings, MT
Manager/Salesman, 11/04 - present
Manage own jewelry business. Sell jewelry at wholesale and retail levels.
Negotiate prices with customers. Handle all finances and bookkeeping.

West Miami Jewelry, Miami, FL
Manager, 1/97 - 11/04
Managed a retail jewelry store. Oversaw all aspects of sales, purchasing, and
bookkeeping. Supervised two employees.

Pelencho Travel, Chicago, IL
Travel Consultant, 4/93 - 1/97
Sold airline tickets and tour packages. Advised customers on travel plans.
Handled ARC reports to airline corporations.

EDUCATION:
Interamerica Business Institute, Billings, MT
2/03 - present
Major: Business Management

New World Institute, Chicago, IL
1992 - 1993
Certificate, Travel Consultant

References available on request.

FUNCTIONAL RESUME

EUGENE HARRIS

2900 Greynolds St. • Deltona, FL 32725
(813) 555-2929 • eugeneharris@xxx.com

SKILLS & ACHIEVEMENTS:

- Developed and installed financial structure and controls of a new company, which facilitated the sale of the business at a substantial profit within six years.
- Directed the design and installation of a computerized financial reporting system for a growth company without any increase in personnel.
- Supervised the design and installation of a tied-in standard cost system that identified scrap and labor variances, thereby saving $200,000.
- Strengthened inventory controls that resulted in a $260,000 decrease in inventory and minimal inventory adjustments.
- Decreased accounting staff by 20 percent by converting manual posting to computerized job-order system.
- Originated a "sound alarm" bulletin that tracked percentage-of-completion of jobs, thereby controlling costs.
- Decreased auditing fees by 15 percent by initiating a procedure for preparation schedules for year-end working papers.
- Initiated and installed financial procedures for a highly profitable turnaround situation.

EMPLOYMENT HISTORY:

Finance Director 2001 - present	Amalgamated Systems Miami, FL
Controller 1996 - 2001	Charles T. Murrow, Inc. New York, NY
Controller/Treasurer 1985 - 1995	The Morris Company Detroit, MI
Controller 1978 - 1985	Adams Cable, Inc. Detroit, MI

EDUCATION:

Baruch College of City University, Peoria, IL
B.A. in Accounting, 1978

Pace University, Detroit, MI
Computer Studies Certificate, 1995

REFERENCES:

Furnished on request.

- Always try to fit your resume on one page. If you are having trouble with this, you may be trying to say too much. Edit out any repetitive or unnecessary information, and shorten descriptions of earlier jobs where possible. Ask a friend you trust for feedback on what seems unnecessary or unimportant. For example, you may have included too many optional sections. Today, with the prevalence of the personal computer as a tool, there is no excuse for a poorly laid out resume. Experiment with variations until you are pleased with the result.

Remember that a resume is not an autobiography. Too much information will only get in the way. The more compact your resume, the easier it will be to review. If a person who is swamped with resumes looks at yours, catches the main points, and then calls you for an interview to fill in some of the details, your resume has already accomplished its task. A clear and concise resume makes for a happy reader and a good impression.

There are times when, despite extensive editing, the resume simply cannot fit on one page. In this case, the resume should be laid out on two pages in such a way that neither clarity nor appearance is compromised. Each page of a two-page resume should be marked clearly: the first should indicate "Page 1 of 2," and the second should include your name and the page number, for example, "Julia Ramirez—Page 2 of 2." The pages should then be paper-clipped together. You may use a smaller type size (in the same font as the body of your resume) for the page numbers. Place them at the bottom of page one and the top of page two. Again, spend the time now to experiment with the layout until you find one that looks good to you.

Always show your final layout to other people and ask them what they like or dislike about it, and what impresses them most when they read your resume. Make sure that their responses are the same as what you want to elicit from your prospective employer. If they aren't the same, you should continue to make changes until the necessary information is emphasized.

Proofreading

After you have finished typing the master copy of your resume and before you have it copied or printed, thoroughly check it for typing and spelling errors. Do not place all your trust in your computer's spellcheck function. Use an old editing trick and read the whole resume backward—start at the end and read it right to left and bottom to top. This can help you see the small errors or inconsistencies that are easy to overlook. Take time to do it right because a single error on a document this important can cause the reader to judge your attention to detail in a harsh light.

Have several people look at the finished resume just in case you've missed an error. Don't try to take a shortcut; not having an unbiased set of eyes examine your resume now could mean embarrassment later. Even experienced editors can easily overlook their own errors. Be thorough and conscientious with your proofreading so your first impression is a perfect one.

We have included the following rules of capitalization and punctuation to assist you in the final stage of creating your resume. Remember that resumes often require use of a shorthand style of writing that may include sentences without periods and other stylistic choices that break the standard rules of grammar. Be consistent in each section and throughout the whole resume with your choices.

RULES OF CAPITALIZATION

- Capitalize proper nouns, such as names of schools, colleges, and universities; names of companies; and brand names of products.

- Capitalize major words in the names and titles of books, tests, and articles that appear in the body of your resume.

- Capitalize words in major section headings of your resume.

- Do not capitalize words just because they seem important.

- When in doubt, consult a style manual such as *Words into Type* (Prentice Hall) or *The Chicago Manual of Style* (The University of Chicago Press). Your local library can help you locate these and other reference books. Many computer programs also have grammar help sections.

RULES OF PUNCTUATION

- Use commas to separate words in a series.

- Use a semicolon to separate series of words that already include commas within the series. (For an example, see the first rule of capitalization.)

- Use a semicolon to separate independent clauses that are not joined by a conjunction.

- Use a period to end a sentence.

- Use a colon to show that examples or details follow that will expand or amplify the preceding phrase.

- Avoid the use of dashes.

- Avoid the use of brackets.

- If you use any punctuation in an unusual way in your resume, be consistent in its use.

- Whenever you are uncertain, consult a style manual.

Putting Your Resume in Print

You will need to buy high-quality paper for your printer before you print your finished resume. Regular office paper is not good enough for resumes; the reviewer will probably think it looks flimsy and cheap. Go to an office supply store or copy shop and select a high-quality bond paper that will make a good first impression. Select colors like white, off-white, or possibly a light gray. In some industries, a pastel may be acceptable, but be sure the color and feel of the paper make a subtle, positive statement about you. Nothing in the choice of paper should be loud or unprofessional.

If your computer printer does not reproduce your resume properly and produces smudged or stuttered type, either ask to borrow a friend's or take your disk (or a clean original) to a printer or copy shop for high-quality copying. If you anticipate needing a large number of copies, taking your resume to a copy shop or a printer is probably the best choice.

Hold a sheet of your unprinted bond paper up to the light. If it has a watermark, you will want to point this out to the person helping you with copies; the printing should be done so that the reader can read the print and see the watermark the right way up. Check each copy for smudges or streaks. This is the time to be a perfectionist—the results of your careful preparation will be well worth it.

The Cover Letter

Once your resume has been assembled, laid out, and printed to your satisfaction, the next and final step before distribution is to write your cover letter. Though there may be instances where you deliver your resume in person, you will usually send it through the mail or online. Resumes sent through the mail always need an accompanying letter that briefly introduces you and your resume. The purpose of the cover letter is to get a potential employer to read your resume, just as the purpose of the resume is to get that same potential employer to call you for an interview.

Like your resume, your cover letter should be clean, neat, and direct. A cover letter usually includes the following information:

1. Your name and address (unless it already appears on your personal letterhead) and your phone number(s); see item 7.

2. The date.

3. The name and address of the person and company to whom you are sending your resume.

4. The salutation ("Dear Mr." or "Dear Ms." followed by the person's last name, or "To Whom It May Concern" if you are answering a blind ad).

5. An opening paragraph explaining why you are writing (for example, in response to an ad, as a follow-up to a previous meeting, at the suggestion of someone you both know) and indicating that you are interested in whatever job is being offered.

6. One or more paragraphs that tell why you want to work for the company and what qualifications and experiences you can bring to the position. This is a good place to mention some detail about

that particular company that makes you want to work for them; this shows that you have done some research before applying.

7. A final paragraph that closes the letter and invites the reviewer to contact you for an interview. This can be a good place to tell the potential employer which method would be best to use when contacting you. Be sure to give the correct phone number and a good time to reach you, if that is important. You may mention here that your references are available upon request.

8. The closing ("Sincerely" or "Yours truly") followed by your signature in a dark ink, with your name typed under it.

Your cover letter should include all of this information and be no longer than one page in length. The language used should be polite, businesslike, and to the point. Don't attempt to tell your life story in the cover letter; a long and cluttered letter will serve only to annoy the reader. Remember that you need to mention only a few of your accomplishments and skills in the cover letter. The rest of your information is available in your resume. If your cover letter is a success, your resume will be read and all pertinent information reviewed by your prospective employer.

Producing the Cover Letter

Cover letters should always be individualized because they are always written to specific individuals and companies. Never use a form letter for your cover letter or copy it as you would a resume. Each cover letter should be unique, and as personal and lively as possible. (Of course, once you have written and rewritten your first cover letter until you are satisfied with it, you can certainly use similar wording in subsequent letters. You may want to save a template on your computer for future reference.) Keep a hard copy of each cover letter so you know exactly what you wrote in each one.

There are sample cover letters in Chapter 6. Use them as models or for ideas of how to assemble and lay out your own cover letters. Remember that every letter is unique and depends on the particular circumstances of the individual writing it and the job for which he or she is applying.

After you have written your cover letter, proofread it as thoroughly as you did your resume. Again, spelling or punctuation errors are a sure sign of carelessness, and you don't want that to be a part of your first impression on a prospective employer. This is no time to trust your spellcheck function. Even after going through a spelling and grammar check, your cover letter should be carefully proofread by at least one other person.

Print the cover letter on the same quality bond paper you used for your resume. Remember to sign it, using a good dark-ink pen. Handle the letter and resume carefully to avoid smudging or wrinkling, and mail them together in an appropriately sized envelope. Many stores sell matching envelopes to coordinate with your choice of bond paper.

Keep an accurate record of all resumes you send out and the results of each mailing. This record can be kept on your computer, in a calendar or notebook, or on file cards. Knowing when a resume is likely to have been received will keep you on track as you make follow-up phone calls.

About a week after mailing resumes and cover letters to potential employers, contact them by telephone. Confirm that your resume arrived and ask whether an interview might be possible. Be sure to record the name of the person you spoke to and any other information you gleaned from the conversation. It is wise to treat the person answering the phone with a great deal of respect; sometimes the assistant or receptionist has the ear of the person doing the hiring.

You should make a great impression with the strong, straightforward resume and personalized cover letter you have just created. We wish you every success in securing the career of your dreams!

Chapter 5

Sample Resumes

This chapter contains dozens of sample resumes for people pursuing a wide variety of jobs and careers in business management.

There are many different styles of resumes in terms of graphic layout and presentation of information. These samples represent people with varying amounts of education and experience. Use them as models for your own resume. Choose one resume or borrow elements from several different resumes to help you construct your own.

KRISTINE HINCH

5222 38th St.
Washington, DC 20013
(202) 555-2003
kristinehinch@xxx.com

OBJECTIVE:

Personnel Management.

WORK EXPERIENCE:

Avery Publishing Company, San Francisco, CA
Payroll Specialist, 2004 - present
  Determine job grading system. Evaluate jobs. Maintain employee budget.
  Conduct performance appraisals. Decide wage increases and adjustments.
  Set salary ranges. Write job descriptions. Coordinate compensation surveys.
  Gather data on vacations, sick time, and leaves of absence. I manage these
  tasks using a variety of office software, including Lotus Notes and
  Microsoft Office.

EDUCATION:

University of California at Santa Barbara
Bachelor's degree in Economics, 2003

Personnel Management Institute
Harrison University, Seattle, WA
Summer 1999

HONORS:

UCSB Economics Scholarship, 1999 - 2003
Elected Student Government Treasurer, 2002
Gamma Kappa Phi Honorary Society, 2001 - 2003

REFERENCES:

Available upon request.

Johanna Farac

152 S. Fedner Drive
Omaha, NE 73802
(402) 555-9000 (Day)
(402) 555-6712 (Evening)
johannafarac@xxx.com

Job Objective

A position as a management trainee with a major bookstore retail chain selling to all trade areas.

Work Experience

Crown Books, Inc., Omaha, NE
Assistant Sales Manager, 2003 - present
Sell books, wait on customers, fill mail orders, handle special orders, and take care of returned merchandise. Contribute to window displays. Handle the placing of ads for a major advertising campaign. Represent store at conventions.

Fern Books, Fernwood, NE
Salesperson, 1999 - 2001
Sold books to customers, filled special orders, organized and arranged inventory. Handled customer complaints and special requests.

Education

Omaha High School, Omaha, NE

- Graduated June 2001
- Ranked 12th in a class of 320
- Worked in student bookstore four years

References

Provided on request.

YOLANDA RICHARDS

6600 Manhattan Ave.
Brooklyn, NY 10090
(718) 555-9656
yolandarichards@xxx.com

JOB OBJECTIVE:
Vice President of Focus Lens, Inc.

PROFESSIONAL EXPERIENCE:
Focus Lens, Inc., New York, NY
Regional Manager, 2002 - present
- Sell custom-designed point-of-purchase elements and product displays.
- Research target areas and develop new account leads. Place advertising in national publications and on websites. Make sales presentations to potential customers. Participate in lens industry trade shows.

Redheart Lawn Co., Forest Lawn, NY
District Sales Manager, 1999 - 2002
- Planned successful sales strategies to identify and develop new accounts.
- Supervised seven sales representatives. Increased sales by at least 20 percent in each of my four years. Researched and analyzed market conditions to seek out new customers. Wrote monthly sales reports.

Ace Office Supply Co., Brooklyn, NY
Account Executive, 1996 - 1999
- Managed accounts in the New York metropolitan area. Expanded customer base 30 percent in four years. Maintained daily contact with customers by telephone to ensure good customer/company relations. Wrote product information flyers and distributed them through a direct-mail program.

EDUCATION:
Northwestern University, Evanston, IL
M.B.A. with honors, 1995
Drake University, Des Moines, IA
B.A. in Accounting, 1992

PROFESSIONAL MEMBERSHIPS:
Brooklyn Sales Association, 2001 - present
New York Merchants Group, 1999 - present

REFERENCES
Available upon request.

CAROLYN JAMESON

6900 Market St. #455
San Francisco, CA 91009
(415) 555-2990
(415) 555-3939
carolynjameson@xxx.com

EMPLOYMENT OBJECTIVE:

A management position in an American/Continental restaurant in the greater San Francisco area.

EMPLOYMENT HISTORY:

Le Boufant, San Francisco, CA
Assistant Manager, 2004 - present
Assist in supervision of general food service in a 65-table restaurant. Oversee breakfast and luncheon kitchen and dining staffs. Develop menus in conjunction with the chef. Handle bookkeeping.

Hilton Hotel, Oakland, CA
Assistant Banquet Manager, 2001 - 2004
Organized and planned banquets and private parties for various business meetings, community events, wedding receptions, and other personal events. Chose meals, music, and decorations along with hosts.

Smiley's Bar & Grill, San Francisco, CA
Waitress, 1999 - 2001

EDUCATION:

American Restaurant Institute, Los Angeles, CA
Certificate in Restaurant Management, 2003
Santa Monica Junior College, Santa Monica, CA
Associate's degree in Food Services, 1998

PROFESSIONAL MEMBERSHIPS:

Bay Area Restaurant Association, 2004 - present
Neighborhood Development Council, 1999 - 2002

REFERENCES:

Available upon request.

GERALD ROBERT SCAMPI

4890 W. 57th St. • New York, NY 10019
(212) 555-3678 • geraldscampi@xxx.com

• JOB OBJECTIVE
Vice President of Promotion for a communications company.

• PROFESSIONAL EXPERIENCE
2002 - present
ATLANTIC RECORDS, New York, NY
<u>Promotion Manager.</u> Develop and execute all marketing strategy for record promotion in New York, New Jersey, and Massachusetts. Interface with sales department and retail stores to ensure adequate product placement. Attend various company-sponsored sales, marketing, and management seminars.

1992 - 2001
IRS RECORDS, Studio City, CA
<u>Promotion Manager.</u> Planned all marketing strategy for record promotions in the southeast United States. Worked closely with sales and touring bands to ensure product visibility in the marketplace.

1990 - 1992
WLAV RADIO, Grand Rapids, MI
<u>Music Director/Morning DJ.</u> Played CHR music. Made TV appearances and public events appearances for the station. Organized and staffed station's news department. Promoted to Music Director after one year.

1985 - 1990
WGLT RADIO, Atlanta, GA
Served as Program Director, Music Director, and News Director during my tenure.

• EDUCATION
Columbia College, Chicago, IL
Attended 1984 - 1985
Studied audio engineering.

References available on request.

CHRISTOPHER BERNARD SMALLS

600 W. Porter St. #5
Las Vegas, NV 89890
(514) 555-3893
christophersmalls@xxx.com

OBJECTIVE

A position as a management trainee in a manufacturing company.

EDUCATION

University of Nevada, Las Vegas, NV
Bachelor of Science in Business
Expected June 2006

HONORS

Dean's List four semesters
Dornburn Scholarship
UNLV Undergraduate Business Award

ACTIVITIES

President, Kappa Beta Fraternity
New Student Week Committee
Homecoming Planning Committee
Captain, Tennis Team

WORK EXPERIENCE

Porter Rand & Associates, Seattle, WA
Sales Intern, 2005
Assisted sales staff in the areas of research, demographics, sales forecasts, identifying new customers, and promotion.

University of Nevada, Las Vegas, NV
Research/Office Assistant, 2002 - 2004
Researched and compiled materials for department professors. Arranged filing system and supervisor's library. Organized department inventory.

SPECIAL SKILLS

Experience using Microsoft Office 2000 software programs.

References available.

WILLIAM ROBERT GARRETT

5050 W. Palatine Road
Little Rock, AR 72201
(501) 555-3789 (Home)
(501) 555-1000 (Work)
williamgarrett@xxx.com

JOB OBJECTIVE

A management-level position in computer sales where I can use my sales and technical experience in the computer industry.

RELEVANT EXPERIENCE

SALES

- Handled sales accounts for northwest suburban Little Rock area.
- Expanded customer base by 25 percent during my tenure.
- Conducted field visits to solve customers' problems.
- Maintained daily contact with customers to ensure good customer/company relations.
- Wrote product information flyers and sales manual.
- Contributed content to company website.

TECHNICAL

- Installed and maintained operating system.
- Defined and oversaw network lists and tables.
- Coordinated problem solving with phone companies.
- Performance-tuned subsystems and networks.
- Planned and installed new hardware and programming techniques.

SYSTEMS ANALYSIS

Documented procedures for mechanization of payroll department.
Created standards and procedures for main accounting system.
Developed test procedures for re-verification of new application.
Developed distribution lists, user IDs, and standards for electronic mail system.

EMPLOYMENT HISTORY

MICROTECH COMPUTERS, Little Rock, AR
Account Executive, 1997 - present

EMPLOYMENT HISTORY (continued)

APPLE COMPUTERS, Berkeley, CA
Technical Support Specialist, 1990 - 1997

DATALOG, INC., St. Louis, MO
Systems Analyst, 1987 - 1989

EDUCATION

UNIVERSITY OF CHICAGO, Chicago, IL
M.S. in Mathematics, 1987
Honors graduate

Northwestern University, Evanston, IL
B.S. in Communications, 1984

PROFESSIONAL AFFILIATIONS

Computer Sales Association
Citizens for a Cleaner Environment

SEMINARS

Microtech Sales Seminars
Apple Technical Workshops

References available on request.

GEORGIA SADEN
453 Franklin Ave.
San Diego, CA 94890
(619) 555-3489
georgiasaden@xxx.com

OBJECTIVE
A management position in marketing where I can use my promotion and public relations experience.

WORK EXPERIENCE
JUST PASTA INC., San Diego, CA
Marketing Director, 2004 - present
Developed a successful marketing campaign for a restaurant chain. Initiated and maintained a positive working relationship with radio, print, and online media. Implemented marketing strategies to increase sales at less profitable outlets, including getting reviews on blogs to increase word-of-mouth exposure. Designed a training program for store managers and staff to introduce basic marketing concepts.

GREAT IDEAS CARPET CLEANING CO., Dallas, TX
Marketing Representative, 2000 - 2004
Demonstrated carpet cleaners in specialty and department stores. Reported customer reactions to manufacturers. Designed flyers and advertising to promote products. Made frequent calls to retail outlets.

REBO CHIPS, INC., Chicago, IL
Assistant to Sales Manager, 1995 - 2000
Handled both internal and external areas of sales and marketing, including samples, advertising, and pricing. Served as company sales representative and sold potato chips to retail outlets.

EDUCATION
University of Illinois at Chicago, Chicago, IL
B.A. Marketing, 1994

SEMINARS
San Diego State Marketing Workshop, 2004, 2005
Sales and Marketing Association Seminars, 2002

References available on request.

JEFFREY CROSS

4901 Main St. #242
Evanston, IL 60202
(847) 555-6362
jeffreycross@xxx.com

JOB OBJECTIVE

Seeking a position as manager of a housewares department of a major department store where I can use my talents as a manager and a salesperson.

ACHIEVEMENTS

Promoted from customer service representative to salesperson to assistant manager in housewares at Marshall Field's. Managed a staff of five, including hiring, job training, and supervision. Helped to reorganize inventory control methods. Assisted customers in choosing housewares and in interior design matters. Combined managerial and sales talents to increase department sales figures.

WORK EXPERIENCE

Marshall Field's, Skokie, IL
Assistant Manager, 2004 - present
Salesperson, 2002 - 2004
Customer Service Representative, 2000 - 2002

Peters Hardware, Evanston, IL
Stock Clerk, Summers 1998 - 2000

EDUCATION

Evanston High School, Evanston, IL
Graduated June 2000

Top 25 percent of class
Student Council Representative
Animal Rights Committee

Oakton Community College, Des Plaines, IL
Various night courses, including Sales Techniques and Retail Management

AHA Seminar, "Selling Housewares," 2004

REFERENCES

Provided upon request.

JANIS DARIEN

345 W. 3rd St. #42
Boston, MA 02210
Telephone: (617) 555-3291
E-mail: janisdarien@xxx.com
Website: www.janisdarien.com

JOB OBJECTIVE:

To obtain a position as a Marketing Management Trainee.

EDUCATION:

Boston University, Boston, MA
B.A. degree in Economics, 2005
Dean's List four quarters
3.45 GPA in major field
3.21 GPA overall
Homecoming Planning Committee

Pursuing graduate studies toward a master's degree in Marketing at Boston
University, Evening Division.

Central High School, Evansville, IN
Graduated 2001
Top 10 percent of class
Business manager and coordinator of student newspaper
Vice President of senior class
Student Council
Pep Club

WORK EXPERIENCE:

Lewis Advertising Agency, Boston, MA
Marketing Assistant, Summer 2004
Assisted Marketing Manager in promotion, product
development, and demographic analysis.

Paterno Marketing, Boston, MA
Telephone Interviewer, Summer 2000 - 2003

SPECIAL SKILLS:

Fluent in French.
Familiar with PC hardware and software, including Adobe.

REFERENCES:

Available on request.

LYDIA REGAN BOMSON

8000 East Fifth Avenue • Silver Springs, MD 04890
(202) 555-8398 • lydiabomson@xxx.com

OBJECTIVE:
A management position in the textile manufacturing industry.

EMPLOYMENT HISTORY:
Interco., Washington, DC
Regional Sales Manager, 2001 - present
> Manage sales of all product lines in eastern markets for a leading manufacturer of cotton products. Represent five corporate divisions of the company with sales in excess of $2 million annually. Direct and motivate a sales force of 12 in planned selling to achieve company goals.

Robertson Co., Miami, FL
District Manager, 1996 - 2001
> Acted as sales representative for the Miami metropolitan area. Built both wholesale and dealer distribution substantially during my tenure. Developed monthly sales plans that identified necessary account maintenance and specific problems that required attention.

Western Office Products, Inc., Sarasota, FL
Assistant Sales Manager, 1987 - 1996
> Handled both internal and external areas of sales and marketing, including samples, advertising, and pricing. Served as company sales representative and sold a variety of office supplies to retail stores.

EDUCATION:
Miami University, Miami, FL
B.A. in English, 1985

SEMINARS:
American Business Association Seminars, 2001 - 2004

REFERENCES:
Available on request.

MARION ZARET

3333 W. 57th St. • Apartment 12E • Brooklyn, NY 12909
(718) 555-2323 • (718) 555-4999 • marionzaret@xxx.com

OBJECTIVE:
Public relations director for soft drink company.

WORK EXPERIENCE:
Coca-Cola, Inc., New York, NY
National Sales Manager, 2005 - present
Account Manager, 2003 - 2005
Assistant Account Manager, 2002 - 2003
Personnel Assistant, 2000 - 2002
Receptionist, 1998 - 2000
   Managed a sales/marketing staff that included account managers and
   sales representatives. Monitored and studied the effectiveness of a
   national distribution network. Oversaw all aspects of sales/marketing
   budget. Designed and executed direct-mail program that identified
   marketplace needs and new options for products. Conceived ads,
   posters, and point-of-purchase materials for products.

Public relations–related experience:
   Represented company to clients and retailers in order to present new
   products. Organized and planned convention displays and strategy.
   Initiated and published a monthly newsletter that was distributed to
   current and potential customers.

EDUCATION:
American University, Washington, DC
B.A. in English, 1997

SEMINARS:
American Marketing Association Seminars, 1999 - 2002
Coca-Cola Internal Sales Workshops, 2000 - 2002
Soft Drink Industry Conventions

SPECIAL SKILLS:
Computer literate in Virtual Basic. Experience using WordPerfect and
Lotus software.

References available on request.

YOSHEMA MUNO

7640 N. Redden Road   **(708) 555-3908**
Skokie, IL 60076   **(708) 555-2300**
yoshema@xxx.com

JOB OBJECTIVE

A position as manager of a store that sells quality shoes and accessories.

WORK EXPERIENCE

Florsheim Shoes, Skokie, IL
Assistant Manager, 2003 - present
Serve as assistant manager of a quality shoe store with partial supervision of eight salespeople. Research customers' buying habits and preferences. Handle promotions and mailings for special sales and in-store events. Help to increase sales through personal attention to customer needs.

Handleman Shoe Store, Lincolnwood, IL
Salesperson, 2001 - 2003
Sold high-quality women's shoes at an exclusive store. Named top salesperson of 2002 and 2003. Maintained a clean, attractive store area and organized inventory.

Florsheim Shoes, Chicago, IL
Salesperson, 1998 - 2001
Sold shoes. Assisted customers in making purchase decisions. Organized and maintained stock and inventory. Helped with window displays.

EDUCATION

Stevenson Community College, Chicago, IL
Attended two years. Majored in political science.

Calumet High School, Calumet, IL
Graduated 1998. Won science award.

REFERENCES

Available on request.

DONALD R. CRUMP

5001 Providence St. • Washington, DC 02930
(201) 555-8000 • (201) 555-3894
donaldcrump@xxx.com

OBJECTIVE:
A position as marketing manager for Graphics, Inc.

PROFESSIONAL EXPERIENCE:
Burger World, Inc., Washington, DC
Marketing Director, 2002 - 2005
Developed a successful marketing campaign for a fast-food chain. Initiated and maintained a positive working relationship with radio, TV, and print media. Implemented marketing strategies to increase sales at less profitable outlets. Designed a training program for store managers and staff.

Hi Fidelity Stereo Co., Newark, NJ
Marketing Representative, 1997 - 2002
Demonstrated electronic equipment in stereo and department stores. Reported customer reactions to manufacturers. Designed flyers and advertising to promote products. Made frequent calls to retail outlets.

Interco, New York, NY
Sales Representative, 1990 - 1997
Identified clients' needs and problems and assured them of personal attention. Resolved service and billing problems. Delivered sales presentations to groups and individuals. Identified potential customers and established new accounts.

EDUCATION:
Georgetown University, Washington, DC
B.S. Evening Division, 1996
Major: Marketing
Minor: English

SEMINARS:
Washington Sales and Marketing Convention, 2001, 2002
National Marketing Association Seminar, 1999 - 2004

SPECIAL SKILLS:
Fluent in Spanish. Able to program in C++.

REFERENCES:
Available on request.

HENRY JAZZINSKI

3000 Big Mile Road   (214) 555-8888 (Daytime)
Dallas, TX 84038   (214) 555-3839 (Evening)

henryjazzinski@xxx.com

OBJECTIVE
A management position in the sales and marketing field.

ACHIEVEMENTS
Sales
- Increased watch sales from $3 million to $12 million during the past six years.
- Introduced new and existing product lines through presentations to marketing directors of major manufacturers.
- Developed 15 new accounts. Supervised five sales agencies throughout the United States and Canada.

Marketing
- Developed new products and expanded product line from watches to other accessories, resulting in increased sales.
- Researched the watch market to coordinate product line with current fashion trends. Increased company's share of the market through improved quality products.

WORK HISTORY
- Culture Shock Watch Co., Dallas, TX
  Vice President of Sales and Marketing, 2002 - present
- Nabisco Food Co., San Francisco, CA
  Sales and Product Manager, 1993 - 2002
- Avis, Inc., Los Angeles, CA
  Sales Representative, 1988 - 1993

EDUCATION
University of Southern California, Los Angeles, CA
B.S. in Business Administration, 1987

SEMINARS
Dallas Sales and Marketing Seminar, 1999 - 2003
National Marketing Association, 2001 - 2003

References available on request.

RUTH M. DAVID
572 First Street • Brooklyn, NY 11215
(212) 555-6328 • ruthdavid@xxx.com

Education
Princeton University, Princeton, NJ
Degree expected: M.B.A., June 2006
Class rank: Top 25 Percent
Honors: Associate Editor, Business Journal

University of Wisconsin, Madison, WI
B.A. in Political Science, May 2002
Honors: Dean's List, Marching Band, Drill Instructor, Section Leader, Residence Hall
Council President

Business Experience
International Business Machines, White Plains, NY
Intern/Sales, 6/05 - 9/05
> Assisted in PC Sales Division. Worked to promote distribution to retail
> outlets. Helped to coordinate product demonstration program used
> throughout the country.

Other Experience
Citizen Action Group, New York, NY
Field Manager, 6/04 - 9/04
> Promoted citizen awareness of state legislative process and issues of toxic
> waste, utility control, and consumer legislation. Demonstrated effective
> fund-raising and communication methods to the canvass employees.
> Developed employee motivation program that increased employee
> productivity.

University of Wisconsin, Madison, WI
Resident Assistant, Office of Residential Life, 8/02 - 5/04
> Administered all aspects of student affairs in university residence halls,
> including program planning, discipline, and individual group counseling.
> Directed achievement of student goals through guidance of the residence
> hall council. Developed and implemented university policies.

University of Wisconsin, Madison, WI
Staff Training Lecturer, 8/01 - 11/02
> Conducted workshops for residence hall staff on counseling and effective
> communication.

References available on request.

MATTHEW R. CLARKSON

1251 S. Maple Ave.
Des Moines, IA 52909
(515) 555-4999 (day)
(515) 555-3429 (evening)
matthewclarkson@xxx.com

OBJECTIVE:
Manager of the hardware department of a major department store.

RELEVANT ACHIEVEMENTS:
- Promoted from customer service representative to salesperson and then to assistant manager in hardware at Sears in Des Moines.
- Managed a staff of six, including hiring, job training, and supervision.
- Helped to reorganize inventory control methods.
- Assisted customers in choosing and using hardware products.
- Combined managerial and sales talents to increase department sales.

EMPLOYMENT HISTORY:
Sears, Des Moines, IA
Assistant Manager, 2001 - present
Salesperson, 1999 - 2001
Customer Service Representative, 1997 - 1999

Sam's Hardware, West Petersville, IA
Stock Clerk, Summers 1995 - 1997

EDUCATION:
Des Moines Township High School, Des Moines, IA
Graduated June 1995
Top 25 percent of class
Student Council Secretary
Homecoming Committee

Redbrook College, Des Moines, IA
Various night courses, including Retail Sales Management and Supervisory Techniques.

REFERENCES:
Available on request.

RAMON HERVEZ

4742 N. Lawndale • Kalamazoo, MI 49001
(616) 555-2574 • ramonhervez@xxx.com

OBJECTIVE:

To obtain a management position where I can employ my creative and organizational skills to increase store visibility and profitability.

WORK EXPERIENCE:

Wood's Video, Kalamazoo, MI
Assistant Manager, 2005 - present
Serve as assistant manager of a full-service video store with partial supervision of five salespeople. Research customers' buying habits and preferences. Handle promotions and mailings for special sales and in-store events. Increase sales by personally attending to customer needs.

Johnson Florists, Portage, MI
Salesperson, 1998 - 2005
Sold flowers. Greeted and advised customers. Generated repeat business by encouraging customers to return. Entered data in computer to track inventory. Handled returns and orders from distributor. Designed displays for store.

Mita Co., Battle Creek, MI
Sales Representative, 1993 - 1998
Sold office copiers to businesses and schools in the greater Chicago area. Serviced copiers. Maintained good customer relations through frequent calls and visits. Identified potential customers.

EDUCATION:

Western Michigan University, Kalamazoo, MI
Attended two years.
Majored in business.

Central High School, Kalamazoo, MI
Graduated 1993.
Won math award.

REFERENCES:

Available on request.

PETER SIMMONS

678 Park Street #546
Noblesville, IN 46060
(317) 555-1223
petersimmons@xxx.com

OBJECTIVE:

To obtain an executive position in marketing with an emerging company that is dedicated to a long-term program.

EXPERIENCE:

5/02 - Present   **DCS SOFTWARE, INC., Noblesville, IN**
                  Senior Partner

- Contingency marketing agency
- Designed marketing strategies for local and national companies
- Directly responsible for meeting payroll of 25 full-time employees
- Improved sales for one company by more than 25 percent in a 12-month period
- Developed marketing programs for corporations

1/97 - 5/02   **BLAUVELT ENGINEERS, New York, NY**
                  Regional Sales Manager

- Business communications systems
- Set regional sales record in six months
- Procured 10 national accounts
- Exceeded company goals for the 1997 fiscal year
- Developed sales marketing program for the northwest regional area

8/93 - 1/97   **EDWARDS AND KELCEY, Livingston, NJ**
                  Marketing Director

- Implemented international marketing program
- Promoted from sales executive to marketing director
- Increased sales more than 100 percent in a 12-month period
- Developed database and resold directly

EDUCATION:

Stevens Institute of Technology, Hoboken, NJ
Bachelor of Arts degree in Technical Marketing Design, 1993

References available on request

MEGAN T. PHILLIPS
4332 S. Bridgefield Lane • San Diego, CA 92138
(619) 555-3472 • (619) 555-3678

JOB OBJECTIVE:
A challenging position where I can put my knowledge and experience to work by combining high-volume selling of major accounts with my ability to develop an effective sales force.

EMPLOYMENT HISTORY:
Tribor Industries, San Diego, CA
Regional Sales Manager, 2003 - present
Manage sales of various product lines in western markets for a leading producer of high-quality linens. Represent several corporate divisions of a company with sales in excess of $3 million annually. Direct and motivate a sales team of 12 representatives in planned selling to achieve and surpass company goals.

District Manager, 1998 - 2003
Acted as sales representative for the San Diego metropolitan area. Expanded wholesale and dealer distribution by 80 percent during my tenure. Promoted to Regional Sales Manager after five years' service.

American Office Supply, Chicago, IL
Assistant to Sales Manager, 1994 - 1998
Handled internal and external sales and marketing, including samples, advertising, and pricing. Served as company sales representative and sold a range of office supplies to retail stores.

EDUCATION:
University of Michigan, Ann Arbor, MI
B.A. Business Administration, 1993
Major: Management

SEMINARS:
National Management Association Seminar, 2002
Purdue University Seminars, 1995, 1996

PROFESSIONAL MEMBERSHIPS:
Sales and Marketing Association of San Diego
National Association of Market Developers

REFERENCES:
Available upon request.

MARION THERESA OPPEREN
2301 E. 5th St. • Seattle, WA 98121
(206) 555-2900 (Day) • (206) 555-2810 (Evening)
marionopperen@xxx.com

OBJECTIVE
Personnel administration position with a growing, innovative company

SKILLS & ACHIEVEMENTS
LABOR RELATIONS
• Oversaw all labor relations between corporation and union.
• Worked with the personnel department to plan labor policy, negotiate
  contracts, review hiring practices, and maintain records.
• Participated in grievance committees. Advised Vice President of Personnel
  on legal matters.
• Supervised a staff of 10 employees.

PERSONNEL ADMINISTRATION
• Supervised a staff of eight interviewers and testers for hiring of office and
  warehouse personnel.
• Assisted Personnel Manager with all department operations.
• Oversaw all records for warehouse personnel.
• Developed a successful training and evaluation program for all company
  employees.

EMPLOYMENT HISTORY
Teledine Electronics, Inc., Seattle, WA
Industrial Relations Manager, 2003 - present

Peperillo's Pasta Co., Moline, IL
Assistant Personnel Manager, 1998 - 2003

George Noffs Storage Co., Moline, IL
Administrative Intern, 1997 - 1998

EDUCATION
University of Illinois, Urbana, IL
Juris Doctor, 1998
Admitted to the Illinois Bar Association, 1998

Kansas College, Wichita, KS
B.S. in Management, 1994

REFERENCES
Provided on request.

SARA STEVENS

332 E. Geobert Rd.
Terre Haute, IN 48930
(317) 555-3890
sarastevens@xxx.com

JOB OBJECTIVE:

Manager of a flower shop.

WORK EXPERIENCE:

TERRY'S FLOWERS, Terre Haute, IN
Assistant Sales Manager, 2004 - present
- Sell flowers, wait on customers, fill phone orders, handle special orders, and design window displays. Handle the placing of ads for a major advertising campaign.
- Represent store at conventions. Create and maintain spreadsheet of customer information.

AVANT BOOKS, Indianapolis, IN
Retail Clerk, 2001 - 2004
- Sold books to customers, filled special orders, and arranged inventory. Handled customer returns and special requests.

EDUCATION:

REVERS HIGH SCHOOL, Indianapolis, IN
Graduated June 2003.
Ranked 15th in a class of 250.
Worked in student bookstore for four years.

REFERENCES:

Available on request.

GEORGE PASTERNECK

1119 S. Figueroa Ave.
Miami, FL 33303
(305) 555-6766
georgepasterneck@xxx.com

OBJECTIVE

A management position in a large finance company.

EDUCATION

University of Miami, Miami, FL
Graduate School of Business Administration
M.B.A. expected June 2006
Concentration: Finance
Finance Club
Student Advisory Board

Boston University, Boston, MA
B.A. in Economics, 2002
Summa Cum Laude
Phi Beta Kappa
Student Government Vice President

WORK EXPERIENCE

Studebaker & Bostwick, Miami, FL
Financial Accounting Intern, 2004
- Participated in standard accounting, credit approval, budgeting, and variance analysis.
- Handled bank balances and money management.

First Florida Bank, Ft. Lauderdale, FL
Commercial Loan Intern, 2002
- Oversaw accounts in the automated teller system. Provided financial data to commercial account officers. Handled the collection of arrears.

Boston University, Boston, MA
Assistant, Accounts Payable Department, 2001 - 2002
- Assisted with bookkeeping, check requests, and disbursements. Billed invoices. Tracked accounts receivable and accounts payable.

References available upon request.

REBECCA ROBINSON

1801 Kirchoff Rd.
Rolling Meadows, IL 60007
(708) 555-3839
rebeccarobinson@xxx.com

JOB OBJECTIVE
Public Relations Director for Hot Fun Sunglasses Co.

ACCOMPLISHMENTS & ACHIEVEMENTS
◆ Managed a sales/marketing staff that included account managers and sales representatives.
◆ Represented company to clients and retailers.
◆ Monitored and studied the effectiveness of a national distribution network.
◆ Organized and planned convention displays and strategy.
◆ Designed and executed direct-mail campaign that identified marketplace needs and new options for products.
◆ Oversaw all aspects of sales/marketing budget.
◆ Conceived ads, posters, and point-of-purchase materials for products.
◆ Initiated and published a monthly newsletter that was distributed to current and potential customers.
◆ Handled design and programming for www.hotfunsunglasses.com website.

WORK HISTORY
Hot Fun Sunglasses Co., Schaumburg, IL
National Sales Manager, 2004 - present
Account Manager, 2001 - 2004
Assistant Account Manager, 1998 - 2001
Research Assistant, 1996 - 1998
Secretary, 1992 - 1996

EDUCATION
Indiana University, Bloomington, IN
B.A. in Economics, 1992

SEMINARS
National Marketing Association Seminars, 1994 - 1998

SPECIAL SKILLS
Computer programming experience, including HTML, database, and spreadsheet skills.

References available.

★ REBA MALONEY

331 Maple Ave.
Seattle, WA 99449
(206) 555-3893 (home)
(206) 555-4444 (cell)
rebamaloney@xxx.com

★ OBJECTIVE

A management position at a dress shop.

★ WORK EXPERIENCE

AVON DRESS SHOP, Seattle, WA
Assistant Sales Manager, 2004 - present
Sell dresses, wait on customers, advise on style, handle special orders and mail orders, and take care of returned merchandise. Assist in the design of window displays. Oversee the placement of ads for a major advertising campaign. Represent store at conventions.

QUALITY BOUTIQUE, Tall Oaks, WA
Salesperson, 2001 - 2004
Sold accessories to customers, filled special orders, organized and arranged inventory. Handled customer returns and special requests. Designed window displays.

★ EDUCATION

TALL OAKS HIGH SCHOOL, Tall Oaks, WA
Graduated June 2001
★ Ranked 14th in a class of 300
★ Worked in student bookstore for four years learning basic business computer and organizational skills
★ Tennis team

★ REFERENCES

Provided on request.

JOHN JAMES HYMAN III

5555 Euclid Avenue
Ft. Lauderdale, FL 33053
(305) 555-8982 (day)   (305) 555-6001 (evening)
johnhyman@xxx.com

OBJECTIVE:
A management position with a machine tool manufacturer where I can apply my abilities and experience in sales and marketing.

WORK EXPERIENCE:
Florida Hydraulics, Inc., Miami, FL
Assistant Sales Manager, January 1999 - present
> Manage a staff of seven sales representatives.
> Supervise the production of a marketing newsletter that has circulation throughout the company. Cowrite the annual marketing plan. Serve as a liaison between sales staff and upper management.

Peaston Machine Tools, Inc., Tampa, FL
Sales Representative, March 1994 - November 1999
> Sold machine tools to business and industry. Wrote articles on sales techniques for monthly newsletter. Handled seven accounts in which sales rose 29 percent during my tenure.

EDUCATION:
B.S. in Civil Engineering
Miami University, Miami, FL, 1994

PROFESSIONAL MEMBERSHIPS:
Society of Civil Engineers, New York, NY
1994 - present

Machine Tools Sales Organization, Chicago, IL
1999 - present

SPECIAL SKILLS:
Fluent in Spanish and French.

REFERENCES:
Available on request.

JOE CAMPOVERDE

9000 N. Evergreen St. • Little Rock, AR 22902
(501) 555-3168 • joecampoverde@xxx.com

JOB OBJECTIVE:

A position as a travel consultant with a long-term goal of management.

WORK EXPERIENCE:

Terrace Travel, Little Rock, AR
Travel Consultant, 2003 - present
- Sell airline tickets and tour packages. Advise customers on travel plans.
- Handle ARC reports to airline corporations. Expert at using Travelbox software.

Joe's Jewelry, Inc., Little Rock, AR
Manager/Salesman, 1999 - 2003
- Managed own jewelry business. Sold jewelry at wholesale and retail levels. Negotiated prices with customers. Handled all finances and bookkeeping.

Savannah Jewelry, Savannah, GA
Manager, 1996 - 1999
- Managed a retail jewelry store. Oversaw all aspects of sales, purchasing, and bookkeeping. Supervised two employees.

EDUCATION:

International Travel School, Little Rock, AR
2001 - 2002
Certificate, Travel Consultant

Savannah University, Savannah, GA
Attended 1994 - 1996
Area of concentration: business management

SPECIAL SKILLS:

Hands-on experience using System One and Sabre.

References available on request.

MICHELLE WOODS

1201 W. Porter Ave.
Oak Park, IL 60302
(708) 555-9000
(708) 555-9492
michellewoods@xxx.com

OBJECTIVE
Vice President of Operations at Osco Drug Co.

WORK EXPERIENCE
Osco Drug Co., Oak Park, IL
Manager of Operations, 2000 - present
Supervise marketing, production, distribution, and accounting. Introduced and developed a computer system to provide accurate inventory controls. Achieved efficiency savings of more than $100,000 during system's first year of operation.

Product Manager, 1998 - 2000
Initiated several new products that resulted in high profit margins for the company. Coordinated research, production, and promotional programs. Introduced new packaging concepts.

Regional Sales Manager, 1996 - 1998
Supervised 34 brokers and salespeople. Increased sales 40 percent through special marketing programs. Developed better customer distribution at lower costs.

District Manager, 1995 - 1996
Handled sales in Chicago area. Increased profits 19 percent in my first year. Promoted to Regional Manager after one year.

Jewel Food Stores, Inc., Melrose Park, IL
Sales Representative, 1992 - 1995
Sold to wholesalers and chain stores in the Midwest. Opened many new accounts that previous sales representatives could not open.

OTHER ACHIEVEMENTS
Marketing consultant for private businesses.
Wrote a book on product efficiency.
Contributed to various trade journals.

Page 1 of 2

EDUCATION

University of Michigan, Ann Arbor, MI
B.S., 1990
Major in Business, minor in Economics
Attended seminars at Simmons Institute, Cleveland, OH, and J. L. Kellogg
School of Management, Evanston, IL

PROFESSIONAL MEMBERSHIPS

National Management Association
Lion's Club, Board of Directors
Midwest Sales Affiliates

REFERENCES

Available upon request.

JUAN C. GARCIA

2103 Afton Street
Temple Hill, Maryland 20748
Home (301) 555-2419
juangarcia@xxx.com

EDUCATION:

Columbia University, New York, NY
Majors: Business, Philosophy
Degree expected: Bachelor of Arts, 2006
Grade point average: 3.8
Regents Scholarship recipient
Columbia University Scholarship recipient

EXPERIENCE:

7/05 - 9/05   Graduate Business Library, Columbia University, NY
General library duties. Entered new students and books into computer
system. Reserved and distributed microfiche and other materials.

9/04 - 5/05   German Department, Columbia University, NY
Performed general office duties. Offered extensive information assistance
by phone and in person. Collated and proofread class materials. Assisted
professors in the gathering of class materials.

6/04 - 9/04   Loan Collections Department, Columbia University, NY
Initiated new filing system for the office. Checked arrears in Bursar's
Office during registration period.

9/03 - 5/04   School of Continuing Education, Columbia University, NY
Involved in heavy public contact and general clerical duties.

SPECIAL ABILITIES:

Fluent in Spanish. Currently studying German. Can program in C++.
Excellent research skills.

REFERENCES:

Available on request.

SANDRA L. PEARSON

12 E. Tenth St.
San Francisco, CA 94890
(415) 555-2343
sandrapearson@xxx.com

JOB OBJECTIVE
A management position in cable television advertising sales.

RELEVANT EXPERIENCE
- Sold television ad space for four major clients in the automotive industry.
- Served as a liaison between clients and television/radio station salespeople.
- Researched demographic and public buying habits for clients.
- Sold space for daytime programming on local TV station.
- Advised station on content and suitability of ads.
- Served as a liaison between station and those purchasing advertising space.

EMPLOYMENT HISTORY
Medialink Advertising Agency, San Francisco, CA
Television Space Sales, September 1999 - June 2005.

KTUT Television, Portland, OR
Television Space Sales, October 1997 - August 1999.

KFTF Radio, Berkeley, CA
Staff Sales Assistant, June 1994 - June 1997.

EDUCATION
B.A. in Communications, University of California at Berkeley, 1994.

HONORS
Seeger Award, Outstanding Communications Senior, 1994
Dean's List, five semesters
Salutatorian, Overland High School, Palo Alto, CA, 1990

References provided on request.

THEODORE WELLINGTON

34 W. Washington Drive • New York, NY 10019
(212) 555-4904
theodorewellington@xxx.com

JOB OBJECTIVE
A senior management position in sales and marketing.

RELEVANT ACHIEVEMENTS
- Introduced new and existing product lines through presentations to marketing directors.
- Developed new products, which resulted in increased sales.
- Increased sales from $3 million to $12 million during the past six years.
- Supervised five sales agencies throughout the United States and Canada.
- Developed 15 new accounts.
- Researched the market to coordinate product line with current trends.
- Increased company's share of the market through improved quality products.
- Oversaw programming and development of company website.

EMPLOYMENT HISTORY
Surf City Skateboard Co., New York, NY
Vice President of Sales and Marketing, 1997 - present

Nike, Inc., San Bernardino, CA
Sales and Product Manager, 1992 - 1997

Vons Ltd., Los Angeles, CA
Sales Representative, 1987 - 1992

EDUCATION
University of Southern California, Los Angeles, CA
B.S. in Marketing, 1985

SEMINARS
Manhattan Sales & Marketing Seminar, 2001 - 2004
National Marketing Association, 1996 - 1997
Webnoize, 1999

REFERENCES
Provided on request.

DARREN SCHWARZWALTER
1001 Park Avenue • New York, NY 11201
(212) 555-1113 • darrenschwarzwalter@xxx.com

JOB SOUGHT
A position in circulation management within the publishing field.

WORK EXPERIENCE
Parker Publishing Co., New York, NY

Circulation Director, 2003 - present

Develop and implement all circulation and related programs. Devise and coordinate merchandise marketing promotions. Oversee subscription promotion, direct response, graphics buying, fulfillment, E-commerce, budgets, agency sales, and newsstand sales.

Northeast Magazine, White Plains, NY

Circulation Director, 1996 - 2003

Directed all circulation areas, direct response programs, agency sales, subscription programs, budgets, and fulfillment. Assisted in advertising and promotion.

Omni Magazine, New York, NY

Assistant Circulation Director, 1992 - 1996

Assisted Circulation Director in circulation activities, including subscription promotion, newsstand, fulfillment, budgets, and direct-response programs.

Sarris & Sarris Publishing, New York, NY

Assistant Operations Manager, 1989 - 1992

Assisted in magazine, book, direct-mail, and merchandise fulfillment services.

EDUCATION
Forest College, Forest Lawn, NY
B.A. in English, 1989
Forest College School of Business Administration
Forest Lawn, NY, 1984

References provided upon request.

LEONARD PHILLIP SCHROEDER

1550 W. Harbor Drive
Milwaukee, WI 53201
(414) 555-1434 (day)
(414) 555-3333 (night)

JOB OBJECTIVE

Marketing manager for a company that manufactures auto parts.

PROFESSIONAL EXPERIENCE

MARKETING
- Researched competitive products to evaluate competitors' strengths and weaknesses.
- Planned a marketing strategy that resulted in a significant increase in accounts.
- Maintained demographic data to ascertain buyer profile.

SALES AND PROMOTION
- Made cold calls and visits to sporting goods retailers, which resulted in increased accounts.
- Visited and serviced existing accounts to encourage continued sales.
- Advised customers on options available to meet a wide range of product needs.
- Handled dealer requests for information and sample products.

EMPLOYMENT HISTORY

Sears Automotive, Inc., Milwaukee, WI
Assistant Sales Manager, 2003 - present
Sales Representative, 2001 - 2003

Teychert Co., Milwaukee, WI
Marketing Assistant, 2000

Royal Crown Cola, Inc., Cicero, IL
Salesperson, 1998 - 2000

Baker's Square Restaurant, Lincolnwood, IL
Waiter, 1997 - 1998

Page 1 of 2

EDUCATION

Southern Illinois University, Carbondale, IL
B.A. in Marketing, 2000

HONORS

Phi Beta Kappa, 2000
Dean's List, 1998 - 2000
Harrison Marketing Scholarship Recipient, 1998, 1999
President, Student Activities Board, 2000

SPECIAL SKILLS

Experience using a variety of word processing, database, and spreadsheet software. Knowledge of German and French.

REFERENCES

Provided on request.

GEORGE T. SNOW

87 Ichiban Ave.
Fairbanks, AK 99191
(907) 555-4951
georgesnow@xxx.com

JOB OBJECTIVE:
Banquet Manager.

SKILLS & ACCOMPLISHMENTS:
FOOD SERVICES
• Directed all kitchen activities.
• Coordinated meal preparation for banquets.
• Planned menus in conjunction with banquet hosts.
• Interacted with caterers.
• Served as liaison to union officials.
• Oversaw parking arrangements for banquets.

MANAGEMENT
• Interviewed and trained kitchen and wait staff.
• Planned work schedules.
• Ordered all food and beverages.
• Maintained emergency backup staff.
• Designed and maintained budgets.

EMPLOYMENT HISTORY:
Fairbanks Feast, Fairbanks, AK
Restaurant Manager, 2001 - present
Assistant Restaurant Manager, 1998 - 2001

James Restaurant, Morrison Hotel, Provo, UT
Assistant Director, 1995 - 1998
Waiter, 1993 - 1995

EDUCATION:
Provo Junior College, Provo, UT
A.S. in Food Service, 1991

References furnished upon request.

PAMELA SUE HUSPERS

pamelahuspers@xxx.com

Permanent Address:
24 South East Hollow Road
Berlin, NY 10951
(518) 555-6057

Temporary Address:
150 Fort Washington Ave.
New York, NY 10032
(212) 738-2498

OBJECTIVE:
A management trainee position in the telecommunications industry.

EDUCATION:
Bachelor of Science, Communications
New York University, New York, NY
Date of Graduation: May 2005
Communications G.P.A.: 3.45
Academic G.P.A.: 3.07

PROFESSIONAL EXPERIENCE:
Volunteer, V.I.T.A. (Volunteer Income Tax Assistance)
Spring 2005
Provided income tax assistance to lower-income and elderly taxpayers who were unable to prepare returns or pay for professional assistance.

Tutor, self-employed
September 2003 - present
Help students to better understand the basic concepts of mathematics.

Cook, Randy's Seafood, New York, NY
Summer 2002
Prepared and cooked assorted seafood dishes. Accounted for deliveries and receiving.

General Laborer and Driver, Jones Construction, Brooklyn, NY
Summers 2001 - 2002
Operated heavy machinery and handled other responsibilities, including delivering materials to and from various job sites.

ACTIVITIES AND HONORS:
• Beta Alpha Psi (Communications Honor Society), 2005
• Dean's List, Fall 2003 & Spring 2004
• AISEC - Association for International Business
• Racquetball and tennis teams

REFERENCES:
Available upon request.

DANIEL KEYS

548 W. Hollywood Way • Burbank, CA 91505

(818) 555-9090 • danielkeys@xxx.com

➤ PROFESSIONAL OBJECTIVE:

An upper-level management position in the record industry where I can employ my sales, marketing, and promotion experience.

➤ PROFESSIONAL BACKGROUND:

Warner Bros. Records, Burbank, CA
Director of Marketing/Jazz Department, 2001 - present
Develop and implement strategic marketing plans for new releases and catalog. Produce reissue packages and samplers, both retail and promotional. Create ad copy. Interface with creative services, national/local print and radio, and Internet sites. Oversee all aspects of sales. Coordinate promotional activities and chart reports.

Immortal Records, Los Angeles, CA
National Sales Manager, 1999 - 2001
West Coast Sales Manager, 1995 - 1999
Increased sales profile, specifically West Coast retailers, one-stops, and racks. Promoted to National Sales Manager where I established sales and promotion programs for the company. Coordinated radio/chart reports.

Specialty Records, Scranton, PA
Sales Representative, 1995
Handled sales, merchandising, and account servicing for LPs and cassettes. Called on major chains and small independent retailers. Promoted new releases and maintained account inventory.

Tower Records, Los Angeles, CA
Manager, 1994 - 1995
Handled sales, merchandising, customer service, product selection and ordering, personnel management, and supervision for a full-line retail outlet.

MCA Records Distribution, Universal City, CA
Sales Representative, 1992 - 1994
Promoted and sold MCA products to Los Angeles and surrounding counties. Designed in-store and window displays. Coordinated media advertising support programs.

➤ EDUCATION:

Berkeley University, Berkeley, CA
B.A., Liberal Arts, 1990

References provided on request.

RANDALL COURY
62 Collins Place #43
New Orleans, LA 33290
(504) 555-3490
(504) 555-3999

OBJECTIVE	A position as manager of a record store.
EMPLOYMENT HISTORY	WEST RECORDS, New Orleans, LA Assistant Manager, 2003 - present Sell records, wait on customers, assist in product selection and ordering, handle special orders and returned merchandise. Design window displays. Oversaw the placement of ads for a major advertising campaign. Represent the store at conventions. Implemented and maintain store website (www.westrecords.com) and e-mail database.
	THE BELT STORE, West Lake, LA Salesperson, 2000 - 2002 Sold accessories to customers, filled special orders, organized and arranged inventory. Handled customer returns and special requests. Assisted in the design of window displays.
EDUCATION	EAST CENTRAL HIGH SCHOOL, New Orleans, LA Graduated June 2000 Ranked 12th in a class of 200 Tennis Team Homecoming Committee
REFERENCES	Available on request.

Sara Woods

4400 Sunset Blvd. • Los Angeles, CA 90028
(213) 555-8989 • (213) 555-4950
sarawoods@xxx.com

Objective
A position in sales management.

Achievements
■ Planned successful strategies to identify and develop new accounts.
■ Increased sales by at least 20 percent each year as District Sales Manager.
■ Researched and analyzed market conditions in order to seek out new customers.
■ Developed weekly and monthly sales strategies.
■ Supervised seven sales representatives.
■ Conducted field visits to solve customer complaints.
■ Maintained daily customer contact to ensure good customer/company relations.
■ Wrote product information flyers and distributed them through a direct-mail program.

Work Experience
Southern California Fruit Co.
Los Angeles, CA
District Sales Manager, 2004 - present

L.A. Freight Co.
Los Angeles, CA
Account Executive, 2002 - 2004

Handlemen & Associates
Santa Rita, CA
Sales Representative, 2001 - 2002

Education
University of Colorado, Boulder, CO
B.A., 2001
Major: Management
Minor: Political Science
G.P.A.: 3.3/4.0

Professional Memberships
Southern California Sales Association, Treasurer, 2002 - 2004
Los Angeles Chamber of Commerce, 2002 - present

Special Skills
Experienced with Lotus and WordPerfect.
References provided upon request.

WOODROW
ARTHUR
TONEY

76 N. Washington Blvd.
Houston, TX 72009
(714) 555-4890
woodrowtoney@xxx.com

OBJECTIVE:
A management trainee position in the manufacturing industry.

WORK EXPERIENCE:
R&G Sugar, Inc., Houston, TX
Salesman, 2000 - 2005
Sold refined sugar products to retail businesses. Named top salesman of 2004.
Maintained good customer relations by identifying customer needs. Trained
new sales representatives and advised them on effective selling techniques.

Popson Camera Co., Milwaukee, WI
Salesman, 1995 - 2000
Sold cameras to retail outfits in the south suburban Milwaukee area. Increased
territory sales by 85 percent in five years. Demonstrated and planned specific
uses for products in various offices. Maintained constant contact with accounts.

EDUCATION:
Popson Sales Training Course, Milwaukee, WI
Summer 2000

Cobert Technical High School, West Allis, WI
Graduated 1995
Football Team, Co-captain

REFERENCES:
Available upon request.

WILLIAM GAVIN

2666 Western Ave. #44

Madison, WI 55590

(414) 555-2029

williamgavin@xxx.com

EDUCATION:

UNIVERSITY OF WISCONSIN, Madison, WI
M.B.A., 2004
Area of Concentration: Accounting

UNIVERSITY OF WISCONSIN, Madison, WI
B.A. in History, 2000, graduated Summa Cum Laude
Gamma Summa Honorary Society
Leopold Scholarship
Areas of Study:
Basic, Intermediate, and Advanced Accounting
Business Law
Cost Accounting
Statistical Methods
Planning and Control
Tax Law
Investments

WORK HISTORY:

WISCONSIN FEDERAL, Madison, WI
Payroll Teller, 2000 - present
Handle transactions with payroll personnel of various companies and
organizations involving the distribution of employee checks.

MARSHALL FIELD'S & CO., Milwaukee, WI
Salesperson, 1996 - 2000
Sold men's clothing at the retail level.

References available

MARK T. CHRISTENSON

65 W. Harrison
Minneapolis, MN 44490
(612) 555-1212 (day)
(612) 555-2901 (night)
markchristenson@xxx.com

JOB OBJECTIVE

Regional Manager for a computer software company.

PROFESSIONAL EXPERIENCE

Sales and Promotion
- Made cold calls and visits to software retailers, which resulted in increased accounts.
- Visited and serviced existing accounts to encourage continued sales.
- Advised customers on options available to meet a wide range of product needs.
- Handled dealer requests for information and sample products.
- Oversaw company's E-commerce.

Marketing
- Researched competitive products to evaluate competitors' strengths and weaknesses.
- Planned a marketing strategy that resulted in a significant increase in accounts.
- Maintained demographic data to ascertain buyer profile.

EMPLOYMENT HISTORY

Assistant Manager, 2003 - present
Thomas Software Inc., Minneapolis, MN

Sales Representative, 2001 - 2003
Quaker & Co., St. Paul, MN

Marketing Assistant, 2000
Salesperson, 1998 - 2000
USA Computer Supplies, Skokie, IL

Waiter, 1997 - 1998
Bennigan's Restaurant, Columbus, OH

EDUCATION
Washington University, St. Louis, MO
B.A. in Business, 2000

HONORS
Phi Beta Kappa, 2000
Honor Roll, 1998 - 2000
Terrance C. Maples Business Scholarship Recipient, 1998, 1999
President, Student Activities Board, 2000

SPECIAL SKILLS
Experience using a variety of word processing, database, and spreadsheet software for both PC and Mac.

REFERENCES
Provided on request.

DEREK STRONG

1501 N. Polk Ave. • Iowa City, IA 52240 • (217) 555-5552
derekstrong@xxx.com

POSITION DESIRED:

Financial Management Director.

SKILLS & ACHIEVEMENTS:

RESEARCH

❱ Conducted consumer surveys.
❱ Coordinated policy formulation.
❱ Developed advertising concepts and strategies.
❱ Controlled transportation and distribution costs.

DEVELOPMENT

❱ Handled costs forecasting and pricing policies.
❱ Implemented costing techniques.
❱ Oversaw research and development budgeting.
❱ Conducted feasibility studies.

PLANNING

❱ Handled long- and short-range financial forecasting.
❱ Managed capital investment opportunities.
❱ Made financial projections.
❱ Directed tax reductions and budgets.

ANALYSIS

❱ Involved in statistical methodologies and analysis.
❱ Administered trend analysis.
❱ Conducted media evaluations and survey designs.

WORK EXPERIENCE:

Control Data, Inc., Springfield, IL
Senior Financial Analyst, 2002 - present
Warner Co., Jackson, MS
Financial Analyst, 1988 - 2002

EDUCATION:

Howard University, Washington, DC
M.A. in Financial Planning, 1998
Thelonious College, Jackson, MS
B.A. in Economics, 1986

References available on request.

TAWANA SANDRA GOLDMAN

4553 N. Alamo Avenue
Dallas, TX 74667
(216) 555-8908
tawanagoldman@xxx.com

OBJECTIVE:
Financial manager for a travel company.

EXPERIENCE:
American Airlines, Inc., Dallas, TX
Customer Service Coordinator, 2001 - present
Sell reservations for domestic flights, hotels, and car rentals.
Market travel packages through travel agencies. Negotiate airline
and hotel discounts for customers. Devise itineraries and solve
customers' travel-related problems.

Salt Lake Travel, Salt Lake City, UT
Travel Agent, 1997 - 2001
Handled customer reservations for airlines, hotels, and car rentals.
Advised customers on competitive travel packages and prices.
Interacted with all major airlines, hotel chains, and car rental
companies.

EDUCATION:
University of Illinois, Urbana, IL
B.A. in Business, 1997

SPECIAL SKILLS:
- Hands-on experience using most travel-related computer
  systems, including Sabre.
- Working knowledge of German, French, and Polish.

REFERENCES:
Available on request.

PAULA STEVENSON

2782 W. 57th St. • Washington, DC 02390
(202) 555-8908 • (202) 555-7200
paulastevenson@xxx.com

OBJECTIVE:
A management position in the import business.

WORK EXPERIENCE:
Sandler Imports, Washington, DC
Manager of Operations, 2002 - present
Manage 10 field representatives. Handle information dissemination and distribution. Codesigned a full-color catalog. Place advertising in major trade publications. Promote products at trade shows and on company website. Maintain inventory status reports and personnel records.

HTO Publishing Co., Owings Mills, MD
Distribution Assistant, 1997 - 2002
Developed new distribution outlets through cold calls and follow-up visits. Increased distribution in my district by 45 percent over a three-year period. Coordinated a direct-mail program that increased magazine subscriptions by 120 percent.

Eastman Kodak Co., Atlanta, GA
Sales Representative, 1992 - 1997
Sold office copiers to businesses and schools in the greater Atlanta area. Serviced copiers. Maintained good customer relations through frequent calls and visits. Identified potential customers.

EDUCATION:
Georgetown University, Washington, DC
B.S. in Communications, 1991

PROFESSIONAL MEMBERSHIPS:
National Association of Importers
DC Community Association
Lion's Club

REFERENCES:
Available on request.

THOMAS GEORGE UHR
4220 Woodridge Drive • Ft. Lauderdale, FL 30898
(305) 555-2898 (Home) • (305) 555-2900 (Work) • thomasuhr@xxx.com

OBJECTIVE

A career in business management in the technical industry.

SKILLS & ACHIEVEMENTS

MANAGEMENT
- Hired consultant engineers and trained them in technical and interpersonal communications.
- Oversaw the expansion of the department.
- Developed a career path strategy with management that was successfully implemented.

ADMINISTRATION
- Supervised seven employees responsible for running the central communications operation.
- Handled the inventory of the product development department.
- Developed and wrote a proposal that led to the implementation of a streamlined communications system.

PERSONNEL
- Trained more than 300 people, including vice presidents, managers, salespeople, and field engineers.
- Developed course objectives and a task analysis for trainees.
- Oversaw personnel evaluations and made appropriate recommendations.

EMPLOYMENT HISTORY

Porter & Hawkins, Inc., Miami, FL
General Manager, Communications Department, 2004 - present
Assistant Director of Personnel, 2000 - 2004
Technical Instructor, 1997 - 2000
Technician, 1982 - 1997

EDUCATION

University of Florida, Miami, FL
B.A. in Management, Evening Division, 1999
Miami-Dade Community College, Miami, FL
Certificate in Electronics, 1981

REFERENCES

Available upon request.

GEORGE ALONZO
1711 N. Gurman Ave.
Atlantic City, NJ 02110
(609) 555-8971
georgealonzo@xxx.com

CAREER OBJECTIVE: Restaurant Management.

EXPERIENCE:
Food Service
- Supervised kitchen staff of eight.
- Conducted business with a local catering service.
- Interviewed, hired, and trained student food service workers.
- Catered banquets.
- Served dining patrons as a waiter.

Management
- Ordered and maintained inventory of all food and beverages for a college cafeteria.
- Planned budget and strictly adhered to it.
- Organized work schedules for student workers.
- Managed computerized purchasing, bookkeeping, and payroll.

Food Preparation
- Assisted in the preparation of meals for 90 children and adults at a summer camp.
- Planned meals for 250 resident students.

EMPLOYMENT HISTORY:
Szabo Food Service/Jersey College, Atlantic City, NJ
Food Service Director, 2002–present

Jersey College, Atlantic City, NJ
Assistant Cafeteria Director, 1997–2002

North Shore Children's Camp, White Cloud, MI
Dining Hall Director, 1996–1997

Paco's Restaurant, Atlantic City, NJ
Waiter, 1995

Tacky's, Garden City, NJ
Busboy, 1994

EDUCATION:
Jersey College, Atlantic City, NJ
B.S. in Business, June 1998

References furnished on request.

HAROLD C. JONES

Bobb Hall, 6 W. Allis Drive • Room 34 • Pittsburgh, PA 28920
(404) 555-2384 • haroldjones@xxx.com

OBJECTIVE:
Position in sales management.

EDUCATION:
University of Pittsburgh, Pittsburgh, PA
Bachelor of Arts in Economics
Expected June 2006

HONORS:
Pitt Honorary Scholar
Pennsylvania Honor Society
Freshman Economics Scholarship, 2004

ACTIVITIES:
Student Government
Freshman Advisor
Homecoming
Planning Committee
Basketball Team

WORK EXPERIENCE:
Nabisco, Inc., Philadelphia, PA
Sales Intern, 2005
Assisted sales staff in research, demographics, sales forecasts, identifying
new customers, and promotion.

University of Pittsburgh, Pittsburgh, PA
General Office, Registrar, 2003
Processed transcript requests. Entered registrations into database.
Provided information to students.

SPECIAL SKILLS:
Able to translate Spanish.
Exemplary skills using Microsoft Word, Excel, and Access software
programs.

REFERENCES:
Available on request.

REVA POPERMAN

UCLA • Snadler Hall • 144 Glendon Ave.
Los Angeles, CA 90289
(310) 555-2384 • revapoperman@xxx.com

CAREER OBJECTIVE
A position in the field of Human Resources.

EDUCATION
UCLA, Los Angeles, CA
Bachelor of Arts in Business
Expected June 2006

HONORS
Phi Beta Kappa
Dean's List, four semesters
Peter J. Tolbrook Award, 2004

ACTIVITIES
President, Student Government
Freshman Advisor
Homecoming Planning Committee
Volleyball Team

WORK EXPERIENCE
NBC, Inc., Burbank, CA
Human Resources Intern, 2005
Assisted Human Resources Director in personnel acquisition and
evaluation. Received and filed resumes. Administered tests to
prospective employees. Set up appointments for interviews.

UCLA, Los Angeles, CA
Research/Office Assistant, 2003 - 2004
Researched and compiled materials for department professors.
Arranged filing system and supervisor's library. Organized department
inventory.

SPECIAL SKILLS
Fluent in Spanish. Experience using FileMaker Pro, Access, Adobe
Acrobat, and Microsoft Office.

References available on request.

PEREGRINE C. WATERS

33301 Rondo Dr.   (602) 555-3920
Tempe, AZ 77799   (602) 555-2222

peregrinewaters@xxx.com

OBJECTIVE

A management position in an accounting firm.

SKILLS & ACCOMPLISHMENTS

- Handled yearly and quarterly accruals and reconciliations.
- Processed several hundred invoices per day.
- Supervised several employees.
- Oversaw up to 50 vendor adjustments and inquiries per day.
- Monitored expenses.
- Processed and routed checks.
- Audited vendor invoices for payment.
- Handled vendor inquiries and adjustments.
- Oversaw bookkeeping, check requests, and disbursements.
- Billed invoices.
- Handled accounts receivable and accounts payable.

EMPLOYMENT HISTORY

BULLOCK'S, Tempe, AZ
Accounts Payable Supervisor, 2004 - present

PETERS, INC., Santa Fe, NM
Accounts Payable Manager, 1999 - 2004

BECKER'S FOODS, INC., Sacramento, CA
Assistant Manager, Accounts Payable, 1991 - 1998

AMERICA WEST, INC., Provo, UT
Billing Coordinator, 1987 - 1991

EDUCATION

TEMPE COMMUNITY COLLEGE, Tempe, AZ
Attended night classes, 1999 - 2000
Studied accounting and advanced accounting.

HANOVER HIGH SCHOOL, Fort Dix, SC
Earned diploma, 1986
Concentration in mathematics

References provided on request.

LINDA S. WOODS

3302 Harbor Drive South #4554
Ft. Lauderdale, FL 33020
(305) 555-8903
(305) 555-9000
lindawoods@xxx.com

WORK EXPERIENCE

South Florida Boat Co., Miami, FL
District Sales Manager, 2004 - present
Plan successful strategies to identify and develop new accounts. Increased sales by at least 20 percent each year (45 percent in 2003). Research and analyze market conditions to seek out new customers. Develop weekly and monthly sales strategies. Supervise seven sales representatives.

Miami Freight, Inc., Miami, FL
Account Executive, 2002 - 2004
Handled sales accounts for southern Florida area. Expanded customer base by 25 percent during my tenure. Conducted field visits to solve customer complaints. Maintained daily contact with customers by telephone to ensure good customer/company relations. Wrote product information flyers and distributed them through a direct-mail plan.

Harrison Pandy, Inc., Denver, CO
Sales Representative, 2001 - 2002
Sold office copiers to businesses and schools in the greater Denver area. Serviced copiers and maintained good customer relations through frequent contact. Identified potential customers for management.

EDUCATION

University of Colorado, Boulder, CO
B.A., 2001
Major: Economics
Minor: Music
G.P.A.: 3.3/4.0

PROFESSIONAL MEMBERSHIPS

South Florida Sales Association, Treasurer, 2001 - 2004
Miami Chamber of Commerce, 2004 - present

REFERENCES

Available on request.

SARAH RESSENELAR

1202 W. North Ave. • Palo Alto, CA 94301
(312) 555-8908 • (312) 555-7200
sarahressenelar@xxx.com

OBJECTIVE:

Retail management.

WORK EXPERIENCE:

Gandy's Shoes, Palo Alto, CA
Assistant Manager, 2001 - present
Serve as assistant manager of a quality shoe store with partial supervision of seven salespeople. Research customers' buying habits and preferences. Handle promotions and mailings for special sales and in-store events. Increase sales through personal attention to customer needs.

Flaherty Jewelers, Palo Alto, CA
Salesperson, 1998 - 2001
Sold jewelry at a fine jewelry store. Greeted customers and advised them. Generated repeat business by encouraging customers to return. Maintained computerized inventory. Handled returns and orders from distributor. Designed displays for store.

Canon Co., Atlanta, GA
Sales Representative, 1993 - 1998
Sold office copy machines to Atlanta businesses and schools. Improved customer relations through frequent calls and service visits. Identified potential customers.

EDUCATION:

Atlanta Community College, Atlanta, GA
Attended two years. Majored in business.

Central High School, Marietta, GA
Graduated 1992. Won math award.

REFERENCES:

Available on request.

DARREN TREVOL

43433 N. Melrose Ave.
Elmhurst, IL 60189
(708) 555-4328
(708) 555-1010
darrentrevol@xxx.com

OBJECTIVE:

Senior vice president of sales and marketing for Vincent Electronics, Inc.

PROFESSIONAL ACHIEVEMENTS:

Marketing

- Researched computer market to coordinate product line with current public tastes and buying trends.
- Developed new approaches to marketing software products, including in-store displays and Internet advertising.
- Organized and planned convention displays and strategies.

Sales

- Introduced new and existing product lines through presentations to major clients.
- Increased sales from $27 million to $50 million in five years.
- Initiated and developed nine new accounts.
- Supervised five sales agencies throughout the United States.

EMPLOYMENT HISTORY:

Vincent Electronics, Inc., Elmhurst, IL
Sales and Marketing Manager, 2004 - present

Porcelana, Inc., Melrose Park, IL
Product Coordinator, 1999 - 2004

Radio Shack, Inc., New York, NY
Sales Representative, 1994 - 1999

EDUCATION:

New York University, New York, NY
B.S. 1994
Major: Business Administration
Minor: Computer Science

REFERENCES:

Available upon request.

PEDRO RENFRO

111 E. 4th St.
Rockford, MI 49341
(616) 555-2931
pedrorenfro@xxx.com

CAREER OBJECTIVE

Assistant Manager of the Accounting Division of a large corporation with the goal of promotion to Manager.

WORK EXPERIENCE

MARSHALL FIELD'S, Kentwood, MI
Accounts Payable Supervisor, 2004 - present
Handle both yearly and quarterly accruals and reconciliations. Supervise seven people. Oversee up to 50 vendor adjustments and inquiries per day. Monitor expenses. Process and route checks.

JONES, INC., Des Moines, IA
Accounts Payable Manager, 1999 - 2004
Oversaw all department activities. Processed several hundred invoices per day. Audited vendor invoices for payment. Supervised 20 people. Handled vendor inquiries and adjustments.

HART'S DETERGENT, INC., Hillsboro, SD
Assistant Manager, Accounts Payable, 1991 - 1998
Processed 400 to 500 invoices per day. Supervised 10 people. Oversaw bookkeeping, check requests, and disbursements.

HANDLEMAN & HANDLEMAN, Fort Dix, SC
Billing Coordinator, 1987 - 1991
Billed invoices. Handled accounts receivable and accounts payable.

EDUCATION

HANOVER HIGH SCHOOL, Fort Dix, SC
Earned diploma, 1986
Concentration in mathematics

References provided on request.

RANDALL KENNEDY

7901 Martella Ave.
New Orleans, LA 29920
(504) 555-2900 (Day)
(504) 555-2810 (Evening)
randallkennedy@xxx.com

WORK EXPERIENCE

Johannson, Inc., New Orleans, LA
Industrial Relations Manager, 2004 - present

> Oversee all labor relations between the corporation and the union. Work with the personnel department to plan labor policy, negotiate contracts, review hiring practices, and maintain records. Participate in grievance committees. Advise Vice President of Personnel on legal matters. Supervise a staff of 10 employees.

Target Discount Stores, Inc., Los Angeles, CA
Assistant Personnel Manager, 1999 - 2004

> Supervised a staff of eight interviewers and testers for hiring of office and warehouse personnel. Assisted Personnel Manager with all department operations. Oversaw all records for warehouse personnel. Developed a successful training and evaluation program for all company employees.

Republic Telephone, Inc., Detroit, MI
Personnel Intern, 1998 - 1999

> Assisted with testing and evaluation of prospective employees. Scheduled interviews. Maintained records.

EDUCATION

University of Michigan, Ann Arbor, MI
Juris Doctor, 1999

Admitted to the Michigan Bar Association, 1999

University of Virginia, Norfolk, VA
B.S. in Management, 1985

REFERENCES

Available on request

ROBERT HAMMOND

16119 Sea View Drive
La Jolla, CA 91201
(619) 555-2221
roberthammond@xxx.com

WORK EXPERIENCE

La Jolla Motel, La Jolla, CA
Manager, 2004 - present
Handled all bookkeeping, payroll, personnel, advertising, and public relations. Developed a successful advertising campaign that increased convention business by 33 percent. Oversaw the implementation of an expansion program.

Assistant Manager, 1999 - 2004
Managed front office, switchboard, groundskeepers, and housekeepers. Hired and trained all personnel. Handled all purchasing and payroll activities. Directed convention and banquet facilities.

Desk Clerk, 1996 - 1999
Handled all registration, reservations, and billing. Informed housekeeping of arrivals and departures of guests. Issued keys and distributed mail.

EDUCATION

San Jose High School, San Jose, CA
Graduated 2001

REFERENCES

Available on request.

JEFFREY P. STOUT

14-44 E. Tyrone Ave.
Omaha, NE 49940
(402) 555-3210
jeffreystout@xxx.com

OBJECTIVE

Business Management

EDUCATION

University of Nebraska, Omaha, NE
M.B.A. expected June 2006
Area of concentration: Financial Management/Accounting Management

Shreveport College, Shreveport, LA
B.A. 2003
Major: Economics
Minor: Political Science

WORK EXPERIENCE

University of Nebraska, Omaha, NE
Analytical Studies Intern, 2004 - present
Collected and organized data for a university finance study.
Conducted library research. Edited draft of final report.

Shreveport College, Shreveport, LA
Resident Hall Assistant, 2001 - 2003
Oversaw all aspects of a college dormitory. Supervised residents, kitchen staff,
and maintenance staff. Served as a liaison to the Student Affairs Office.

References available as requested.

DAVID CHANG

677 Rosewood Drive • San Jose, CA 99002
(510) 555-9090 • davidchang@xxx.com • www.davidchang.com

Goal: A position in business management and development for an Internet start-up.

Education:

June 2004: Master of Business Administration
Florida State University, Jacksonville, FL

June 2002: Bachelor of Arts: Computer Science
University of California, Northridge, CA

Experience:

2004 - Present: Kmart--Operations Analyst & Distribution Management
• Analyze regional distribution center operations and best methods.
• Manage external seasonal distribution center.
• Supervise and work with team members from various departments.
• Prepare and analyze forecasts, budgets, and internal reports.
• Control production by managing volume inflow and outflow.
• Identify opportunities for more efficient and safer product movement.
• Manage the building budget and monitor warehouse expenditures.
• Provide the center with staffing models to ensure optimal staffing levels.
• Assist in recruiting efforts through job fairs, building tours, and interviews.

2002 - Present: MacServ--Business Partner, Consultant, Developer, & Technician
• Provide computer consultation to homes, businesses, and schools.
• Provide regular maintenance and troubleshooting of computer systems.
• Provide training in major software programs for Macintosh and Windows.
• Develop FileMaker Pro applications for businesses.

1999 - 2002: Computer Warehouse--Retail Management, Market Analyst, & Computer Instructor
• Oversaw sales and marketing of all products and services.
• Analyzed market competitiveness and evaluated product performance.
• Communicated and coordinated vendor marketing events and programs.
• Provided customer assistance and resolution of customer complaints.
• Supervised, scheduled, trained, and reviewed up to 60 employees.
• Maintained inventory through store audits and security checks.
• Trained corporations in the operation of computer hardware and software.
• Administered, maintained, and troubleshot store computer network.

References available on request.

• HANNAH P. WEAVER •

14 E. Main St.
Dubuque, IA 33333
(319) 555-8375
hannahweaver@xxx.com

• CAREER OBJECTIVE
Manager of a general bookstore.

• WORK EXPERIENCE
Templeman Books, Dubuque, IA
Manager, 2004 - present
> Manage all aspects of a retail bookstore. Oversee maintenance and selection of inventory. Supervise four employees. Increased sales by 20 percent in first three years. Coordinated design and development of store website.

Templeman Books, Dubuque, IA
Management Trainee, 2003 - 2004
> Learned all aspects of retail bookselling. Sold books, handled customer relations, made sales presentations, designed displays.

Dubuque Camera Shop, Dubuque, IA
Salesperson, 2002 - 2003
> Sold cameras. Processed film orders. Repaired cameras. Assisted customers with their photographic needs.

• EDUCATION
Dubuque College, Dubuque, IA
B.A. in Literature, 2002
• Graduated with honors
• Student Council
• Ski Club

• PROFESSIONAL MEMBERSHIPS
• National Association of Booksellers
• Dubuque Business League

• REFERENCES
Provided upon request.

BRIDGETT TERRY

4444 24th St.
Los Angeles, CA 91809
(213) 555-3411
Bridgett_terry@xxx.com

OBJECTIVE: A management position in personnel administration.

WORK EXPERIENCE: WOODBINE & CO., Los Angeles, CA
Payroll Specialist, 2002 - present
Determine job grading system. Evaluate jobs. Maintain employee budget. Conduct performance appraisals. Decide wage increases and adjustments. Set salary ranges. Write job descriptions. Coordinate compensation surveys. Gather data on vacations, sick time, and leaves of absence.

EDUCATION: UNIVERSITY OF CALIFORNIA AT BERKELEY
Bachelor's Degree in Economics, 2001

PERSONNEL MANAGEMENT INSTITUTE
Lorminon College, Dallas, TX
Summer 1999

HONORS: UCSB Economics Scholarship, 1999 - 2000
Elected Student Government Secretary, 2000
Gamma Kappa Phi Honorary Society, 2000 - 2001

REFERENCES: Available upon request.

CARMEN McRAE

7 E. Magnolia • Atlanta, GA 24990
Phone: (404) 555-7449 • carmenmcrae@xxx.com

ACCOMPLISHMENTS

- Managed administrative activities of a staff of 250.
- Designed improved administrative, clerical, and payroll systems, which resulted in significant savings.
- Oversaw operational studies of the activities and organizational structure of client companies.
- Introduced new purchasing, shipping, and billing procedures.
- Received a high percentage of acceptance on recommendations to upper management.
- Conducted a study of clerical operations in the purchasing department and attained a 20 percent reduction in department budget.
- Revised printing operations, which increased cost efficiency.
- Oversaw the installation of a computer network for the department.

EMPLOYMENT HISTORY

2000 - present	NUMARK SYSTEMS, INC., Atlanta, GA Administrative Manager
1995 - 2000	PARKER LEWIS, INC., New York, NY Accounting Consultant
1989 - 1995	AMERICAN NATIONAL CORP., White Plains, NY Systems Analyst
1986 - 1989	SANDERSON CO., New York, NY Assistant Systems Analyst
1983 - 1986	AT&T, Chicago, IL Accountant

EDUCATION

UNIVERSITY OF GEORGIA, Atlanta, GA
M.B.A., 1982
B.A. in Economics, 1980

REFERENCES

Available upon request.

PATRICK H. McCOY

1701 N. Hampshire Pl.
Miami, FL 33126
(305) 555-3909
(305) 555-9099
patrickmccoy@xxx.com

OBJECTIVE

A management position for a manufacturing business.

WORK EXPERIENCE

NEWMARK FURNACE CO., Miami, FL
Account Executive, 2005 - present
Handled accounts for southern Florida area. Expanded customer base by 28 percent. Conducted field visits to solve customer complaints. Maintained daily contact with customers to ensure good company/customer relations. Wrote product information flyers and distributed them to potential customers.

POTISCO, Terre Haute, IN
Sales Representative, 2001 - 2005
Sold to customers, particularly contractors. Priced bid estimates as required. Oversaw customer and public relations, which helped to build company's image. Set up office procedures where necessary.

HONOCO, INC., Fort Wayne, IN
Sales Representative, 1998 - 2001
Developed and managed new territories. Built sales through calls on physicians, hospitals, retailers, and wholesalers. Developed creative techniques for increasing product sales. Maintained current knowledge of competitive products.

EDUCATION

WHEATON COLLEGE, Wheaton, IL
B.S. in Business, 1997

SEMINARS

Sales and Marketing for the New Millennium
Florida Business Association
Marketing for the Furnace Industry

REFERENCES

Available upon request.

◆ ◆ ◆ ZOE TERRE

839 Wilton St.
Pittsburgh, PA 15100
(412) 555-2902
zoeterre@xxx.com

OBJECTIVE

Management position in a medium- to large-sized accounting firm.

SKILLS & CAPABILITIES

- ◆ Maintained ledgers.
- ◆ Prepared invoices and vouchers.
- ◆ Supplied periodic financial statements.
- ◆ Assisted with internal auditing.
- ◆ Handled accounts payable and receivable.
- ◆ Directed a bookkeeping staff of 10 employees.
- ◆ Experienced with most accounting software.

EMPLOYMENT HISTORY

American Marine Co., Pittsburgh, PA
Accounts Manager, 2000 - present

Parker College, Philadelphia, PA
Assistant Finance Manager, 1997 - 2000

Brentwood & Associates, Philadelphia, PA
Billing Supervisor, 1995 - 1997

NBC, Inc., New York, NY
Bookkeeper, 1994 - 1995

EDUCATION

Peters Junior College, Santa Fe, NM
Business Certificate, 1994

REFERENCES

Available on request.

MARLENE MAREGO

55 E. Wood St.
White Plains, NY 10604
(914) 555-1234
(914) 555-2938
marlenemarego@xxx.com

WORK EXPERIENCE

ITC, INC., White Plains, NY
Executive Vice President, Special Projects, 2001 - present
Manage all administrative operations. Direct the work of several project units simultaneously. Create and implement organizational policy. Plan and develop programs and publications. Design promotional materials. Oversaw website development.

AMERICAN DEVELOPMENT, INC., Miami, FL
Director of Operations, 1994 - 2001
Managed all educational and personnel projects. Prepared proposals for public and private funding. Assisted in technical management functions. Evaluated operations to ensure effective implementation of contractual requirements. Negotiated contracts.

CERTA CORPORATION, Jackson, MS
Account Executive, 1990 - 1994
Handled accounts for all of Mississippi. Expanded customer base by 30 percent during tenure. Conducted field visits to solve customer complaints. Maintained daily contact with customers to ensure good company/customer relations. Wrote product information flyers and distributed them to potential customers.

EDUCATION

NEW YORK UNIVERSITY, New York, NY
M.B.A. with Honors, 1990

UNIVERSITY OF MISSISSIPPI, Jackson, MS
B.A. in Economics, 1988

MEMBERSHIPS

New York Association of Business Executives
National Business Association

REFERENCES

Provided upon request.

JOEL JAMES III

1441 S. Goebert
Providence, RI 00231
(401) 555-1234
(401) 555-3782
joeljames@xxx.com

OBJECTIVE

President of a publishing corporation where I can apply my management, promotion, and marketing experience.

EMPLOYMENT HISTORY

JOHNSON PUBLISHING CORPORATION, Providence, RI
Vice President, Advertising, 1998 - present
Promoted from Marketing Manager to Vice President of Advertising after three years. Managed all phases of publishing properties including:

- Furniture magazine
- Home Improvement Weekly
- Scuba Digest
- Travel Age magazine
- Pharmacy News

Established and developed the first newspaper advertising mat service in the furniture industry. Increased number of distributors and retailers using this service by 55 percent in three years. Improved the effectiveness and volume of all retail advertising.

REBUS PUBLISHING COMPANY, Boston, MA
Advertising Manager, 1989 - 1997
Serviced and developed accounts throughout the eastern United States. Handled advertising for publications in the restaurant industry. Increased sales in my territories every year by at least 21 percent.

TIME MAGAZINE, New York, NY
Assistant Advertising Promotion Manager, 1985 - 1989
Spearheaded original promotion program that increased revenue by 33 percent in two years. Developed new markets. Helped to improve company/customer relations.

X-LARGE CLOTHING, Columbus, OH
Division Sales Manager, 1982 - 1985
Promoted from Salesperson to Division Sales Manager after one year. Organized sampling campaigns and in-store displays. Directed outlets' cooperative advertising and point-of-purchase displays.

EDUCATION
DRAKE UNIVERSITY, Des Moines, IA
B.A. in Economics, 1981
Graduated Phi Beta Kappa
Top 5 percent of class

PROFESSIONAL AFFILIATIONS
ROCKING CHAIR, social and professional organization of the furniture industry
President, 2001 - 2004

INDEPENDENT CLOTHING MANUFACTURERS ASSOCIATION
Board of Directors

PUBLISHERS ASSOCIATION
Advisory Committee

References available upon request.

Gerald Holsten

1205 Maple Avenue

Elsmere, Delaware 19807

Tel. (302) 555-7112

geraldholsten@xxx.com

Objective

Management position in personnel training and development.

Experience

Administration and Development

- Developed intraschool program to improve staff morale and instruction. Created a special program for incoming high school students to facilitate their adjustment to a new environment.
- Administered a remediation and orientation program for newly admitted high school students. Developed and supervised the operations of a college counseling office designed to service 2,000 high school students. Planned career and college fair programs for students. Acted as school liaison to college admissions and financial aid offices and personnel. Published college and career newsletters.

Placement Counseling

- Counseled unemployed clients in a training program for the purpose of job placement. Provided supportive counseling services to clients while they trained for employment. Conducted vocational, career, college, and financial aid counseling and placement for population seeking postsecondary education and training. Provided individual and group counseling and gave large group presentations.

Teaching and Training

- Conducted sessions to improve clients' communication and job interviewing skills. Trained professional and volunteer staff in college admissions and financial aid counseling. Supervised student teachers in their training. Taught and developed curricula in psychology, sociology, and basic learning skills.

Employment History

1999 - Present	Abraham Lincoln High School
1999 (Summer)	GE Employment and Training Systems
1999 - 2003	Thomas Jefferson High School

Education

B.A. (History), 1990, University of Wisconsin
M.S. (Counseling), 1998, University of Wisconsin
Advanced Certificate (Counseling), 1999, University of Wisconsin

Affiliations

American Personnel and Guidance Association, American Psychological Association, Association of Teachers of Social Studies

References

Furnished on request.

**GINA
CAROL
STONE**

5001 Lincoln Drive #2
Marlton, NJ 08053
(609) 555-1200
(609) 555-3893
ginastone@xxx.com

OBJECTIVE
Sales manager of a paper products company.

PROFESSIONAL EXPERIENCE
Harrison Paper Co., Philadelphia, PA
District Sales Manager, 2002 - 2005
Planned successful strategies to identify and develop new accounts. Increased sales by at least 20 percent each year (50 percent in 2003). Researched and analyzed market conditions to seek out new customers. Developed weekly and monthly sales strategies. Supervised seven sales representatives.

Daniel P. Miller & Co., Trenton, NJ
Sales Representative, 1995 - 2002
Developed and managed new territories. Built sales through calls on retailers and wholesalers. Developed creative techniques for increasing product sales. Maintained current knowledge of competitive products. Wrote weekly and monthly sales reports.

Sammy's Best Burger Co., Newark, NJ
Assistant to Sales Manager, 1988 - 1995
Handled both internal and external sales and marketing, including samples, advertising, and pricing. Served as company sales representative and sold a variety of products to retail stores.

EDUCATION
New Jersey State University, Trenton, NJ
B.A. in Botany, 1987
Graduated in top 10 percent of class
Recipient of Floyd T. Harper Botany Scholarship

SPECIAL SKILLS
Programming experience in MySql, C++.
Working knowledge of Russian.

REFERENCES
Available on request.

PATRICK T. KORAN
39392 Broad Street • Meridian, MS 39301 • (601) 555-2929
patrickkoran@xxx.com • www.patkoran.com

OBJECTIVE:
To work for an established Internet company in business management.

EDUCATION:
Master of Business Administration, 2005
Kellogg School of Business, Northwestern University, Evanston, IL
Emphases: International Marketing and Business, Contract Negotiations

Bachelor of Arts--English, 2002
Northwestern University, Evanston, IL
Minor: Business Administration

EXPERIENCE:
Sole Proprietor--eLand, 2003 December - Present
Manage own Internet business. Handle Internet sales, website development, and hosting and digital imaging.

Independent Business Consultant, 1999 May - 2003 May
* Ford Group, Syracuse, NY--Software marketing, research, channel development
* Sam's Travel, Baton Rouge, LA--Digital imaging, desktop publishing
* Hoge Construction Co., Harrisburg, PA--Job costing, strategic analysis
* Fortune's Cookie, Madison, WI--Music management, Web page design, maintenance
* Unistat, Inc., Madison, WI--Market development, value-chain analysis
* Bleecker's, Inc., Chicago, IL--Market survey analysis, strategic analysis

Proposal Marketing Intern, 1996 May - 1998 August
* Alpha Systems, Chicago, IL--Revamped subsidiary reporting method, researched market potential, reviewed congressional activity.

COMPUTER SKILLS:
Adobe Photoshop, Dreamweaver (website editor), Microsoft Office, Publisher, MS Word Suite, Quattro Pro, PageMaker, Harvard, DOS 6.22, Win 3.11, Win 98, Win XP, WWW, Netscape Navigator, Explorer, Free Agent, SalesLogix (relational sales database), Quicken, Zip, CuteFTP to Linux host site, PC-Tools, dBASE IV, Lotus, Eudora 4, Kodak DC260.

References available upon request.

JONATHAN P. KILPATRICK

1400 Mercy Court Drive
Sacramento, CA 95590
(916) 555-3892 (Home)
(916) 555-9000 (Work)
jonathankilpatrick@xxx.com

OBJECTIVE:

Hospital Administrator for a medium- to large-sized hospital.

SKILLS & ACHIEVEMENTS:

- Planned and implemented procedures and policies for several medical facilities.
- Interviewed and hired administrative staffs.
- Oversaw complex activities in operations and finance.
- Prepared and maintained capital project status and budget reports for various hospitals.
- Oversaw the development of an employee training program.
- Wrote an employee manual.
- Managed commercial medical administration for headquarters as well as divisions.
- Interacted and communicated with the Board of Directors.
- Researched and wrote budget reports and proposals.

EMPLOYMENT HISTORY:

Cedar Hospital, Sacramento, CA
Maintenance Control Planner, 2002 - present

Pacific Care Medical Group, San Francisco, CA
Administrative Coordinator, 1998 - 2002

Denver Hospital Collective, Inc., Denver, CO
Director of Planning, 1996 - 1998

Englewood Hospital, Englewood, CO
Assistant Director of Planning, 1993 - 1996
Assistant Administrative Coordinator, 1991 - 1993

Page 1 of 2

EDUCATION:
University of Colorado, Boulder, CO
Master's in Business Administration, 1991
Graduated Summa Cum Laude

Richmond College, Richmond, CA
Bachelor of Arts in English, 1989

PROFESSIONAL MEMBERSHIPS:
California Hospital Association
National Healthcare Administrators Alliance
Sacramento Business Association

REFERENCES
Provided upon request.

CRYSTAL CARTIER

1201 E. Maple Drive
Las Vegas, NV 89901
(702) 555-9346
crystalcartier@xxx.com

CAREER OBJECTIVE

An accounting career leading to management.

SKILLS/ACHIEVEMENTS

- Managed insurance, financial, and brokerage accounting.
- Handled general cost accounting procedures.
- Designed systems for budget and cash flow accounting.
- Oversaw contracts, orders, and vouchers.
- Recorded disbursements, tax payments, and expenses.
- Prepared balance sheets.

WORK HISTORY

HERVEY & CO., Las Vegas, NV
Accountant, 2001 - present

EDUCATION

UNIVERSITY OF NEVADA, Las Vegas, NV
B.A. in Accounting, 1999
C.P.A., 2003

REFERENCES

Provided upon request.

RAMON PARK

16 Port St.
Providence, RI 00727
(401) 555-9020
ramonpark@xxx.com

CAREER OBJECTIVE:
Position as a Credit Manager.

SKILLS & ACCOMPLISHMENTS:
➤ Conducted studies of clients' financial statements and past credit records.
➤ Established credit and collection systems.
➤ Worked with the sales force to develop credit policies.
➤ Oversaw all credit requests.
➤ Supervised and reduced delinquent accounts.
➤ Interviewed applicants for credit and gathered the necessary information for granting credit.
➤ Simplified credit processing system.
➤ Maintained good customer relations.
➤ Reduced turnover in personnel.

EMPLOYMENT HISTORY:

2002 - present	Haring & Andrews, Inc., Providence, RI Credit Manager
1998 - 2002	National Credit, Inc., Boston, MA Assistant Collections Manager
1996 - 1998	Marshall Field's, Chicago, IL Credit Assistant

EDUCATION:

2004	University of Colorado, Boulder, CO B.A. in Accounting
2000	Providence College, Providence, RI Summa Cum Laude, Dean's List
1998	Providence College, Providence, RI Financial Analysis Seminar Financial Management Training

References provided on request.

IVAR T. KOPESKI
501 W. Glendale Blvd.
Kansas City, MO 51132
(816) 555-3524
(816) 555-9090
ivarkopeski@xxx.com

OBJECTIVE
Regional sales manager for a national manufacturer/distributor

---

EXPERIENCE
REB Pharmaceuticals, Kansas City, MO
District Sales Manager, 2002 - present

Direct the selling and servicing of accounts to physicians, pharmacies, and hospitals in the Kansas City area. Increased sales by 50 percent in three years. Initiated an incentive plan that resulted in 21 new accounts. Worked with production department to improve product quality.

Jacobs & Jacobs Advertising, Trenton, NJ
Display Coordinator, 1999 - 2002

Coordinated and supervised the installation of displays in men's clothing stores in the Trenton area. Managed a five-person office in all aspects of display planning and production. Worked to help place the firm in the syndicated display-advertising field.

Mark Shale, Inc., Schaumburg, IL
Retail Store Manager, 1995 - 1999

Promoted from salesperson to assistant manager to manager within two years. Supervised the designing of display for interior and windows. Handled all aspects of personnel, sales promotions, inventory control, and new products. Interacted with corporate management frequently.

EDUCATION
Harper College, Palatine, IL
Attended two years (1993 - 1995) and majored in advertising.
American Institute, Putnam, NJ
Completed course on sales and marketing techniques, 2001

MEMBERSHIPS
American Display Advertisers
Kansas City Sales Association
Kansas City Community Development Association

REFERENCES
Available on request

Sample Cover Letters

This chapter contains sample cover letters for students and graduates who are pursuing a wide variety of jobs and careers in business management.

There are many different styles of cover letters in terms of layout, level of formality, and presentation of information. These samples also represent people with varying amounts of education and work experience. Choose one cover letter or borrow elements from several different cover letters to help you construct your own.

GINA STEVENSON
433 Maple Drive
Hoffman Estates, IL 60035
(708) 555-2341
ginastevenson@xxx.com

May 23, 20__

Lisa Rice
Vice President of Personnel
Laura Ashley, Inc.
111 Commonwealth Avenue
Boston, MA 02215

Dear Ms. Rice:

I am interested in applying for the position of manager of one of your Chicago
area retail stores. Enclosed are my resume and letters of recommendation.
I have been involved in retail sales for more than 20 years and have gained
valuable insight and experience during this time. For the past 10 years, I have
been assistant sales manager at Talbot's in the Woodfield Mall and also the
owner and designer of my own original clothing line, "Gina Designs." My
experience in women's fashion at the retail level well qualifies me for a
management-level position.

I am seeking employment with Laura Ashley because I have admired
Laura Ashley products for many years. I feel that your stores offer the best
in quality and unique women's clothing. This is why I want to be a part of
your organization.

Thank you for taking the time to consider me. I look forward to hearing from
you soon.

Sincerely,

Gina Stevenson

R E V A   P O P E R M A N

UCLA • Snadler Hall • 144 Glendon Ave.
Los Angeles, CA 90289
(310) 555-2384 • revapoperman@xxx.com

January 28, 20__

Helena Borgess
Director of Human Resources
Warner Bros., Inc.
4000 Olive Ave.
Burbank, CA 91505

Dear Ms. Borgess:

This is a letter of inquiry. I would like to know if there are any openings in the Human Resources department at Warner Bros., Inc. My area of interest is the entertainment industry, and that is why I would like to work at Warner Bros.

I will graduate from UCLA with a degree in business in June of this year. Human Resources has been an area of focus in my studies. Last summer I served as an intern in the Human Resources department at NBC, Inc., in Burbank, where I assisted with personnel acquisition and evaluation, administering tests to prospective employees and setting up appointments for interviews. I feel that this internship helped to prepare me for a career in Human Resources within the entertainment industry.

Along with my business education and my experience, I speak fluent Spanish, which I feel is a definite advantage in today's business world.

My resume is enclosed. You may consider me for any openings you might have. I would be happy to interview with you at your convenience.

Sincerely,

Reva Poperman

DAVID P. JENKINS
3663 N. Coldwater Canyon
North Hollywood, CA 90390
(818) 555-3472
(818) 555-3678 cell
davidjenkins@xxx.com

July 29, 20__

Mr. Jeremy Hitleman
Vice President of Sales and Marketing
Sandoval Industries
500 University Drive
Santa Barbara, CA 97809

Dear Mr. Hitleman:

I am writing to you to inquire about the possibility of obtaining a position with
Sandoval Industries as a sales and marketing manager. My special interest in working for your company stems from a desire to expand my experience into the area
of hardware sales. Your company's recent addition of a hardware division brought
Sandoval Industries to my attention.

Currently, I serve as regional sales manager for Tribor Industries where I represent
five corporate divisions with sales in excess of $3,000,000 annually. Prior to this
position, I served as district manager for Tribor. I believe that my sales experience
uniquely qualifies me for a position at Sandoval Industries. I am available for interviews at your convenience. My resume is enclosed.

Sincerely,

David P. Jenkins

PATRICK T. KORAN
39392 Broad Street • Meridian, MS 39301 • (601) 555-2929
patrickkoran@xxx.com • www.patkoran.com

July 11, 20__

Scour.net
345 Maple Drive
Suite 285
Beverly Hills, CA 90210
Attn: James Soner

Dear Mr. Soner:

While visiting your website, I noticed that you are seeking a Director of
Business Development. I would like to have the opportunity to meet with
you to discuss my interest and qualifications for this position.

For the past three years, I have managed my own Internet business, eLand,
handling website development, hosting, digital imaging, and sales. Prior to
that, I served as an independent Internet business consultant for a variety of
companies. My resume is enclosed.

I believe I am capable of managing major activities and projects related to the
pursuit of new business opportunities for Scour.net, analyzing company
strategy, and developing recommendations for new initiatives, alliances,
and partnerships.

Please contact me at your earliest convenience so that I can meet you for an
interview. I look forward to hearing from you soon.

Sincerely,

Patrick T. Koran

April 23, 20__

Harvard Peter Fendi
President, American Finance Co.
4444 E. River Drive
Detroit, MI 33393

Dear Mr. Fendi:

As a recent graduate of The Kellogg School of Business Management at Northwestern University, I am seeking a position in financial management. I met a representative of your company, Jonathon Siveva, at a recruiting seminar at Northwestern a few months ago, and he alerted me to the fact that your company would be hiring M.B.A.s this summer.

At Kellogg, my concentration was in finance. I participated in the Finance Club and served as a member of the Student Advisory Board. My practical experience includes a financial accounting internship at Thomas & Thomas, an internship in the commercial loan department at LaSalle National Bank, and a position in the accounts payable department at Northwestern.

I am enclosing my resume for a more comprehensive picture of my accomplishments and qualifications. I will contact you in the next 10 days to inquire about setting up an interview.

Please feel free to contact me at the number listed below.

Sincerely,

Antonio Cruz
8925 Lake Shore Drive #442
Chicago, IL 60614
(312) 555-2939
antoniocruz@xxx.com

CAROLYN JAMESON

6900 Market St. #455
San Francisco, CA 91009
(415) 555-2990
(415) 555-3939
carolynjameson@xxx.com

March 23, 20___

Giuseppe Spina
Owner & General Manager
Pallermo's Restaurant
238 Market St.
San Francisco, CA 92299

Dear Mr. Spina:

I am responding to your ad in the *San Francisco Examiner* for a manager for your restaurant. My resume is enclosed.

Since 2004, I have been the Assistant Manager at Le Boufant in San Francisco, a 65-table restaurant. I assist in the supervision of food service and oversee breakfast and luncheon kitchen and dining staffs. Prior to this position, I served as Assistant Banquet Manager for the Hilton Hotel in Oakland.

I have a Certificate in Restaurant Management from the American Restaurant Institute and an Associate Degree in Food Services from Santa Monica Junior College.

I am available for an interview anytime. I look forward to speaking with you soon.

Sincerely,

Carolyn Jameson

PATRICK H. McCOY

1701 N. Hampshire Pl.
Miami, FL 33126
(305) 555-3909
(305) 555-9099
patrickmccoy@xxx.com

August 23, 20___

Steven R. Stevens
Red Man Furnace Co.
7892 Collins Ave.
Miami, FL 33102

Dear Mr. Stevens:

I am responding to your advertisement for a Sales Manager in *The Miami Herald* of August 18, 2005. I am interested in such a position, and I am forwarding my resume to you. My sales experience is extensive, going back eight years. As an account executive for Newmark Furnace Co., I have handled sales accounts in the south Florida area and expanded my customer base by 28 percent. Before that, I worked as a sales representative for Potisco in Terre Haute, Indiana, and for Honoco in Fort Wayne, Indiana.

I feel I am qualified for the Sales Manager position. If, after reviewing my resume, you feel the same, please contact me for an interview.

Sincerely,

Patrick H. McCoy

February 18, 20__

Richard Meirs
Manager, Westin Hotel
1131 6th St.
Seattle, WA 98802

Dear Mr. Meirs:

I would like to break into the hotel business, and my long-term goal is management. I am forwarding my resume to you with the hope that you may have an opening on your staff.

In June of 2006 I will graduate from the International School of Business in San Francisco, California, with a Certificate in Hotel Management. My previous work experience includes management of my own cookware business and management of a retail jewelry store.

This work, coupled with my education, has prepared me for a career in hotel management. You will find that I am reliable, hardworking, and competent. Feel free to contact me regarding an interview. Thank you for your time and consideration.

Sincerely,

Tyrell Stevenson
602 S. Texas Ave.
Oakland, CA 94611
(415) 555-3168
tyrellstevenson@xxx.com

DONALD E. THOMPSON
1314 W. Dundee Road
Buffalo Grove, IL 60006
donaldthompson@xxx.com

March 30, 20__

Mr. Henry Corleone
Branch Manager Sales
Datatech Computer Co.
4444 E. Monroe
Grand Rapids, MI 49505

Dear Mr. Corleone:

Please consider me for the position of Assistant Branch Manager of Sales at
Datatech. I am enclosing my resume. I learned of this opening through
Computer Weekly and through my colleague at Microtech.

My experience in the computer industry is extensive and encompasses several
different areas. Currently, I am an Account Executive for Microtech, where
I handle sales accounts for the northwest suburban area. I also contribute
content to the Microtech website. Before Microtech, I worked for IBM in
the capacity of Technical Support Specialist and Systems Analyst.

I believe that my expertise in these diverse areas could enhance Datatech's
talented sales division.

I will call next week to follow up this letter and inquire as to the possibility of
an interview.

Sincerely,
Donald E. Thompson
(708) 555-3909

JEREMY S. PANDY
1441 S. Goebert
Providence, RI 00231

March 11, 20__
Anderson Publishing Inc.
1000 7th Avenue, Suite 1000
New York, NY 10019

Attn: Delores Darnell
       Director of Personnel

Dear Ms. Darnell:

Through your recent press release, I became aware of the departure of your company's president, Myron Strickland. With that in mind, I am forwarding my resume for your consideration in your search for a new president.

With more than 20 years of experience in the publishing industry, including my current position as Vice President of Advertising at Johnson Publishing in Providence, I feel that I have the experience and the industry knowledge to tackle this challenge. My employment history also includes stints with Rebus Publishing and *Time* magazine.

I believe that Anderson Publishing is a company with a great future, and I am convinced that I can help shape that future.

I will follow up this letter with a telephone call next week. I will be in New York City during the week of March 20 and would be happy to meet with you at that time regarding this position.

Thank you for your kind consideration.

Sincerely,

Jeremy S. Pandy
(401) 555-1234
(401) 555-3782
jeremypandy@xxx.com

RANDALL KENNEDY

7901 Martella Ave.
New Orleans, LA 29920
(504) 555-2900 (Day)
(504) 555-2810 (Evening)
randallkennedy@xxx.com

August 23, 20__

Robert Minnelli
President, Dormar Corporation
111 E. State St.
Des Moines, IA 50329

Dear Mr. Minnelli:

I am interested in applying for the position of Senior Personnel Administrator at Dormar. I learned of this opening through a mutual friend, Donald Donner, who works in your accounting division. I am enclosing my resume for this reason.

Currently, Johannson, Inc., employs me as Industrial Relations Manager. I oversee all labor relations with the corporation and the union, work with the personnel department to plan labor policy, review hiring practices, and handle many other related functions. Before my current position, I served as Assistant Personnel Manager at Target Discount Stores.

My interest in your opening stems from a desire to move more in the direction of personnel administration. I believe that my experience in industrial relations gives me a unique perspective as a personnel administrator.

I will be in the Des Moines area from September 2 through September 15. At your convenience, I would like to interview for this position at that time. I will be in touch with you soon.

Sincerely,

Randall Kennedy

JOHN L. RYDER
211 W. Fourth St. #211
Brooklyn, NY 10001
(718) 555-8080
johnryder@xxx.com

June 12, 20__

John Junot
Fidelity Insurance Co.
1440 W. 57th St.
New York, NY 10019

Dear Mr. Junot:

I am responding to your advertisement for an East Coast Branch Manager for Fidelity Insurance Company. As the advertisement requests, I am enclosing my resume and a list of references.

After several years of working as an agent and an adjustor, I am ready to make the move into a management position. I believe that a position of this kind at Fidelity would benefit both your company and my own career development. My vast experience in the insurance industry has prepared me well for this next step in my career.

Please review my resume and let me know if and when you would like me to come to your office for an interview. I look forward to meeting with you.

Sincerely,

John L. Ryder

JANIS DARIEN
345 W. 3rd St. #42
Boston, MA 02210
Telephone: (617) 555-3291
E-mail: janisdarien@xxx.com
Website: www.janisdarien.com

August 23, 20__

David Bascombe III
Sears, Roebuck and Company, Inc.
1000 S. Adams
Chicago, IL 60601

Dear Mr. Bascombe:

I am responding to your job listing for a Marketing Management Trainee that was posted in the placement office at Boston University. I am interested in applying for this position, and therefore I am enclosing my resume with this letter.

I have recently graduated from Boston University with a degree in Economics, and I am anxious to find a position in the marketing field. I am currently working toward a Master's degree in Marketing by taking evening courses.

My work experience includes employment as a Marketing Assistant for Lewis Advertising Agency in Boston and as a Telephone Interviewer for Paterno Marketing.

I will be in the Chicago area the week of September 12. Would it be possible to set up an interview with you during that week? If so, please contact me at your earliest convenience.

Sincerely,

Janis Darien

CRYSTAL CARTIER

1201 E. Maple Drive
Las Vegas, NV 89901
(702) 555-9346
crystalcartier@xxx.com

October 19, 20__

Geraldine Powers
Powers & Powers, Inc.
7700 Main St.
Las Vegas, NV 88883

Dear Ms. Powers:

After spending the last four years as an accountant for Hervey & Co., I am ready to pursue a management position in a larger accounting firm such as yours. Powers & Powers's reputation as a leader in the field has led me to write to you regarding possible management opportunities in your company.

At Hervey & Co., I have managed insurance, financial, and brokerage accounting, handled general cost accounting procedures, and designed systems for budget and cash flow accounting. During the past four years, I have developed solid accounting skills. Now I am ready for something more challenging.

I am enclosing my resume. Please contact me regarding any appropriate openings.

Sincerely,

Crystal Cartier

January 14, 20__

Gekko Publishing, Inc.
1700 Avenue of Industry
Dallas, TX 78989

Attn: Ricardo Montoya
Director of Personnel

Dear Mr. Montoya:

This letter is a response to your advertisement in the *Houston Chronicle*'s classified section. The position of assistant manager of operations for a publisher of Gekko's stature is one that appeals to me. I am enclosing my resume for your consideration.

Currently, I am assistant manager for a small but dynamic publisher in Houston, American National Books, Inc. My experience at American National includes orchestrating market analyses, identifying and meeting clients' needs, maintaining accounts, and establishing new accounts. I also oversee the company's E-commerce on the www.anb.com company website. Before this position, I served as a sales representative for Unico International in Dallas.

I am willing to come to Dallas for an interview at your convenience. I look forward to coming back to work in Dallas, and I am actively seeking employment there now.

Please feel free to contact me at either phone number listed below. I look forward to meeting you and discussing this opportunity.

Sincerely,

Renee Gylkison
8 E. Western Avenue
Houston, TX 75737
(713) 555-8098
(713) 555-6000
reneegylkison@xxx.com

LISA BANFIELD
14 E. Three Penny Road
Detroit, MI 33290
(313) 555-3489
lisabanfield@xxx.com

March 18, 20___

Zan Marketing
500 E. Hubbard Street
Detroit, MI 33909

Attn: Hilda C. Roane

Dear Ms. Roane:

I am interested in applying for your opening for the Marketing Manager position at Zan Marketing. I learned of this opening from your ad in the *Detroit Free Press*.

Currently, I am employed as Marketing Director for 7-Eleven, Inc., in Detroit. Some of my accomplishments at this company include the development of a successful marketing campaign, the implementation of marketing strategies to increase sales at less-profitable outlets, and the designing of a training program for store managers and staff.

Zan's positive reputation is well-known throughout the industry, and I am most interested in helping to perpetuate that reputation.

Please feel free to call me for an interview. My resume is enclosed.

Best regards,

Lisa Banfield

SALLY JOHANSON
3240 Santa Monica Blvd.
Los Angeles, CA 90028
sallyjohanson@xxx.com

December 20, 20__

David G. Sandler
Director of Human Resources
Nessex Motor Co.
12000 Wilshire Blvd.
Santa Monica, CA 90390

Dear Mr. Sandler:

I am interested in applying for the position of Assistant Manager at your
Lexus dealership in Santa Monica. Your ad in the *L.A. Times* alerted me to this
opening.

I am currently a sales representative for Pontiac in Los Angeles where I have
handled sales, market analyses, research, forecasts, and service and billing
problems. I have held this position for three years and am now ready to
explore new challenges in auto sales--assistant manager is one of them. I feel
I am qualified for this job.

Enclosed is my resume. Please take me into consideration. I look forward to
interviewing with you.

Sincerely,

Sally Johanson
(213) 555-9832 (Home)
(213) 555-2121 (Work)

WILLIAM GAVIN

2666 Western Ave. #44

Madison, WI 55590

(414) 555-2029

williamgavin@xxx.com

July 22, 20__

Neil Terpstra
Director of Human Resources
Parker Thomas Accounting, Inc.
7717 E. 3rd Terrace
Milwaukee, WI 55250

Dear Mr. Terpstra:

I am seeking employment in the field of accounting, particularly a position leading to management. My resume is enclosed.

I am a recent M.B.A. graduate of the University of Wisconsin at Madison. My area of concentration at the university was accounting, and my studies included the following:

      Basic, Intermediate, and Advanced Accounting
      Business Law
      Cost Accounting
      Statistical Methods
      Planning and Control
      Tax Law
      Investments

Before my graduate degree, I earned a B.A. in History from the University of Wisconsin, where I graduated Summa Cum Laude and won the Leopold Scholarship.

Considering my preparation, I am ready to begin my career in accounting. I will contact you soon regarding possible job openings. Thank you for your time and consideration.

Sincerely,

William Gavin

Johanna Farac

152 S. Fedner Drive
Omaha, NE 73802
(402) 555-9000 (Day)
(402) 555-6712 (Evening)
johannafarac@xxx.com

September 30, 20__

Susan P. Evers
Federated Books, Inc.
1442 S. 7th Avenue
Omaha, NE 73092

Dear Ms. Evers:

I am responding to your ad in the *Omaha Register* for a management
trainee for your bookstore. My resume and salary requirements are
enclosed as you requested.

All of my life I have had a fascination with books and bookstores. In high
school I worked in the student bookstore all four years, and my work
experience includes stints as a salesperson for Fern Books and as assistant
sales manager for Crown Books in Omaha.

Thank you for your time and consideration. I look forward to hearing
from you and meeting with you soon.

Sincerely,

Johanna Farac

September 22, 20__

Carlos Castillo
Director of Human Resources
Macy's Inc.
5744 N. Franklin Ave.
Miami, FL 33333

Dear Mr. Castillo:

I am responding to your advertisement for a Senior Audit Manager for your company. The ad requested someone with audit experience in a department store. I have such experience and would like to discuss how I can apply my expertise in your business.

For the past nine years, I have served as Audit Manager for Jordan Marsh Company in Ft. Myers, Florida. My responsibilities include overseeing analytical review and verification of financial records, developing audit programs, establishing guidelines for physical distribution of inventory, and evaluation of internal controls. Before Jordan Marsh, I worked for National Textile Co. and Held & Perkins, both in audit and finance.

My resume is enclosed to give you a complete picture of my experience and qualifications.

Please review it and contact me if you would like me to come for an interview. I look forward to hearing from you soon.

Sincerely,

Stephanie Shepard
804 N. Victoria Park Rd.
Ft. Myers, FL 30013
(941) 555-2000 (Work)
(941) 555-5555 (Home)
stephanieshepard@xxx.com

WINONA T. SIMPSON
420 W. Easterly Avenue
Indianapolis, IN 49091
winonasimpson@xxx.com

September 2, 20__

Thomas E. Eagletender
Pizza Hut, Inc.
4200 Bolt Avenue
Indianapolis, IN 48902

Dear Mr. Eagletender:

David Porter of your marketing department informed me that you were looking for
a new P.R. manager for your Midwest office. Therefore, I am sending my resume for
your consideration in regard to this position.

I currently serve as P.R. director for Blockbuster Video in Indianapolis, where I have
been since 1995. Before that I worked as marketing representative for Jeron Stereo
and as P.R. assistant for Kader Advertising.

My accomplishments include developing a successful marketing campaign for
Blockbuster, implementing marketing strategies to increase sales at less profitable
outlets, designing a training program for store managers and staff, and developing
the website.

I believe my resume speaks for itself. I would very much like to meet with you
to discuss this position further. Please contact me at (317) 555-1212 at your
convenience.

Sincerely,

Winona T. Simpson